LOOK TO THE STARS FOR LOVE!

Whether you're aggressive or shy, conservative or kinky, accommodating or stubborn—or anywhere in between!—STARRING YOUR LOVE LIFE will speed you toward success in romance. This fascinating guide reveals the most subtle and intimate facets of your personality, your sensual likes and dislikes, strengths and weaknesses. When you flip to the pages ahead you'll find astrological profiles of all the signs of the zodiac and a unique compatibility guide to the Sun signs in love, including special strategies for attracting the sign of your choice. STARRING YOUR LOVE LIFE will enable you to realize your greatest romantic potential, turning even the most elusive, star-crossed lovers into a match made in heaven!

AUTHOR JONATHAN STERNFIELD provides an invaluable reference for both the experienced and beginning fan of astrology.

The Love Life Guides

#1 Starring Your Love Life
#2 It All Adds Up to Love

STARRING YOUR LOVE LIFE

Jonathan Sternfield

LYNX BOOKS
New York

STARRING YOUR LOVE LIFE

ISBN: 1-55802-041-1

First Printing/August 1988

This book is published by Lynx Books, a division of Lynx Communications, Inc., 41 Madison Avenue, New York, New York, 10010. The name "Lynx" together with the logotype consisting of a stylized head of a lynx is a trademark of Lynx Communications, Inc.

Designed by Sheree L. Goodman

Printed in the United States of America

0 9 8 7 6 5 4 3 2 1

STARRING YOUR LOVE LIFE

An Astrological Guide to Meeting and Mating

STARRING YOUR LOVE LIFE

CHAPTER I

Love's Written in the Stars

If you're anything like the rest of us, love really does make your world go 'round. For the irrepressible romantic in all of us, there's no better place to be than sharing an afternoon at the beach, a candlelight dinner, or even a simple evening at home, in the satisfying company of the person who makes your heart throb out of control. In the warm, happy glow of romance you can discover and explore new sides of yourself and your partner, growing through them and with them. After all, what could be better than life with someone who makes you feel excited, cared-for, and just plain out-of-your-mind happy?

It's no wonder, then, that we spend so much of our time and energy questing for divine love here on Earth.

Once you've had a taste of it, once you know the wonderful feel of that light-headed sensation, love seems as indispensable as the air you breathe.

Wonderful as these experiences might be, however, chances are you find them all-too-rare and fleeting. Frequently, we enter relationships that have undertones of tension, psychological or physical danger, and unsettling instability. Sometimes these affairs take more than they give, and we're left afterward once again perplexed, wondering which trap this was and how we fell into it. More than likely, while these relationships met some of our needs, they came up alarmingly short as regards others. Once the first delicious moments of love have passed, you may realize just how uncontrollable they can be, how idyllic love one day often leads to empty loneliness the next, how dreams of the perfect romance can turn to dust.

These common love sicknesses visit each and every one of us on occasion. The question is, what can you do about it? What can anyone do?

Centuries before Ann Landers or computer-dating services ever began offering their advice to the lovelorn, men and women looked to the stars for answers to the all-important question of romance. From ancient times, astrologers found great order in the celestial patterns and majestic transits of the heavenly bodies, dividing the skies into twelve astrological signs and noting the particular influence of each sign on those who were born into it.

Today, those same influences can make for a surprisingly reliable and insightful means of understanding yourself and knowing which kinds of personalities will best complement your own—which combinations are most likely to result in a happy, long-lasting love relationship. For instance, most Virgos really *are* detail-oriented perfectionists who maintain a "single" outlook even when they're married.

Unlike Newton's law, which states that when you drop an apple you can predict with certainty that it will fall, astro-analysis and forecasting point not to concrete laws, but rather to tendencies, inclinations, and likelihoods. So fate is never really sealed as it is with the falling apple. If you are born under the sign of Aries, for instance, chances are you'll exhibit the enthusiastic, impulsive energy so typical of the Ram. But being an Aries, and having those tendencies, does not glue you to one specific fate *or* to one specific lover. By understanding the characteristics associated with your sign—and with all the signs of the zodiac—you can actively manage your love life, creating and availing yourself of the most advantageous romantic situations for your particular personality.

To maximize the possibilities, both for finding love and keeping it, the first step is to know your own needs and attractions, to clearly understand what it is you bring to a relationship and what you want from it. You must understand who you're looking for, where you might find them, and who it is you're really with once the introductions are over.

More than that, through astrology—and in the pages of this book—you'll acquire an understanding not just of your romantic compatibility with others, but also of how to take advantage of one of the most critical factors in romance: timing. Had your parents not met at just the moment they did, they might never have fallen in love, might never have conceived you. But they *did* meet. And similarly, by being in the right place at the right time, you too may find love, marriage, and family.

You can look to the stars for guidance as to where and when to best test your chances of running into the sensitive Cancer, the dynamic Leo, or the candid and impulsive Sagittarius, with the most favorable results. If you're a Leo, for example, being at the right place at the right time might mean going to that audition your friend mentioned and really giving your acting career another chance. And even though you might not get the part, you do meet a fiery Sagittarian, and are enthralled by his optimistic, freedom-loving ways. He, in turn, is charmed by your proud, sunny disposition and natural abilities of leadership. Your love light ignited, you go off together into the night. You were in the right place physically and psychologically at just the right time to meet your lover.

There is no reason to leave all these coincidences up to fate. And fortunately, a knowledge of astrology can help keep fate on your side.

First, the heavenly science offers your Sun sign, describing your type. Next, there's your birth chart, your cosmic signature at the time of first breath, showing the position of each of the planets and their influence in conjunction with the astrological signs. This mandala is your first and most powerful impression of the heavens, and it is specific for the very spot and moment you were born. It is your unique celestial formula. By studying the celestial influences evidenced in your birth chart, a diagram of your character and your personality will emerge, as well as the ways in which you are likely to use them in meeting life's experiences. You can come to know your real needs and desires, learning to pursue relationships that will fulfill them and steer clear of those that won't.

Empowered with astrological understanding, you can operate to systematically tempt fate, aligning yourself with people and frequenting places likely to yield adventures in mutual attraction. All too often, love is out there, waiting, while we sit at home, yearning. Astrology is a surefire way to connect, where waiting meets yearning . . . with supercharged results.

CHAPTER II

the twelve signs of the zodiac, twelve types of lovers

The zodiac is a mythic band encircling the Earth, and it is divided into twelve sections, in each of which the Sun spends about one month every year. Each of these sections, or Sun signs, has its own special psychological attributes, akin to the Earth's ever-changing seasons.

Naturally, as the light and energizer of our universe, the Sun has great astrological importance. Your Sun sign shows who you are and what character traits are likely to dominate your personality. It signifies your individuality, your purpose in life, and represents your character. According to the characteristics typified by the zodiacal sign under which you were born, your Sun sign strongly influences the way you view the world and how you operate in it. Therefore, an understanding of your Sun sign yields great insight into your nature. And this, in turn, gives you a strong foundation for happiness with others.

Are you aggressive or laid back? Adventuresome or timid? Flamboyant or conservative? More likely to be found on the soccer field or in the library? On the beach or in front of the computer? Your Sun sign will tell you. Suppose you're a Gemini, for example. Do you really differ all that much from a Taurus? You bet you do! For starters, you're almost jumping out of your skin all the time, so fast are the ideas coming to you, whereas your Taurus friend is so low-key about his thoughts that it may seem to you that an idea has never crossed his mind. You can't sit still, while he's very meditative; you're satirical and whimsical; he's the strong, silent type. When the Gemini twin riders of the air meet the earthy Taurus Bull, all of these seemingly opposite traits will most likely surface and collide.

Your Sun sign doesn't tell absolutely everything about you, of course—you'd need your whole birth chart for that, complete with rising sign, Moon sign, and other planetary positions. But the Sun sign alone certainly provides a sufficiently clear picture of you to develop a good snapshot. Some details may be lost, certain characteristics might be out of focus, but nonetheless, the picture will quite clearly represent you . . . or your lover.

Over the thousands of years of astrological history, a great variety of correspondences and associations surrounding the zodiacal signs has developed. The band of the zodiac represents a balanced entity that can be taken apart and examined in different ways. Before examining each individual sign, it is enlightening to note the most important of these associations.

First of all, each Sun sign has a certain *polarity*, either male or female. Six signs are male—Aries, Gemini, Leo, Libra, Sagittarius, and Aquarius. The other six Sun signs—Taurus, Cancer, Virgo, Scorpio, Capricorn, and Pisces—are female. Astrologically speaking, Sun signs with a masculine polarity are energetic and action-oriented, while those with a feminine polarity tend to have a more self-contained strength, and are receptive and responsive.

Naturally, this doesn't mean that men are better off being born under a sign with male polarity, or women under a sign of female polarity. If you're an Aries woman or love one, for instance, do not fear. The Ram's male polarity simply indicates that an Aries female, such as Joan Crawford or Bette Davis, is likely to be more assertive and extroverted than any person born under a sign of female polarity, such as Taurus. Similarly, a Taurus male, Fred Astaire or Bing Crosby, for example, may be more quietly magnetic than many other men.

Second, the signs are divided into four groups by *element*—fire, earth, air, and water. These elements indicate another aspect of personal expression. The Fire signs—Aries, Leo, and Sagittarius—are ardent and spirited, perpetually aflame with their latest idea or adventure. The Earth signs—Taurus, Virgo, and Capricorn—are grounded, practical, and reliable, excellent in carrying out the ideas of others. The Air signs—Gemini, Libra, and Aquarius—are centered in thought and all forms of communication. And the Water signs—Cancer, Scorpio, and Pisces—are the sensitive signs of feeling, intuition, and sometimes, spirituality.

Finally, the *quality* of each sign—either cardinal, fixed, or mutable—indicates the ways in which the sign is likely to respond to his environment. This ranges from the sign's perspective of the world as he finds it, to his nation, state, or city—right on down to his house or apartment. Each person's responses to all these environments are likely to be indicated by the quality of their Sun sign.

The cardinal signs—Aries, Cancer, Libra, and Capricorn—are the most assertive. These are the take-charge types, the initiators and controllers. The fixed signs—Taurus, Leo, Scorpio, and Aquarius—are the most stable and steady of the signs, but they are also the most resistant to change and therefore may have a tendency to get psychologically stuck. The mutable signs—Gemini, Virgo, Sagittarius, and Pisces—are the most flexible and adaptable, undergoing energetic change almost continuously.

The Twelve Lovers

Since Sun signs do not necessarily change at midnight, as dates do, the following Sun-sign dates are approximate. Many of the first days of one sign frequently contain part of the last day of the sign preceding it. If you were born on the cusp—on either the first or last day of any sign, as listed below—you'll need to know the exact time you were born in order to determine your true Sun sign.

ARIES

March 21st through April 20th

Symbol: The Ram
Polarity: Male
Element: Fire
Quality: Cardinal
Ruling Planet: Mars
Part of the Body Ruled: The head
Most Likable Trait: Courage
Key Phrase: I AM
Lucky Day: Tuesday
Lucky Numbers: 1 and 9
Magical Birthstone: Diamond
Color: Red
Cities: Florence, Naples, Verona, Marseilles
Countries: England, Germany, Poland
Flowers: Geranium, Honeysuckle, Sweet Pea
Trees: All thorn-bearing trees
Metal: Iron
Animals Ruled: Sheep and rams

Aries is the sign of the warrior/pioneer, the one who strides to the forefront to take control with new ideas. They are fiery wits, burning brightly with their unquenchable first-of-the-zodiac enthusiasm and zest. Although the Aries lover usually displays a forceful, "me-first" manner, he or she can also be unusually tender and considerate. They need nurturing, that's all. Being the babies of the zodiac, they're brimming with idealistic innocence, and as long as they're supported in mood and action, their love light shines brightly. But cross them or lay them low with some indiscretion, and the rage of Mars, Aries's ruling planet, will be hurled your way, though not for long.

Arians tend to be self-centered, self-confident, willful, and often audacious. Aries rules the head, and accordingly, this sign is known for its headstrong way. Conversely, they can be very vulnerable, and without recognition of their great worth, they are likely to be hurt. The Ram likes to hold court and be authoritative on all matters. Aggressive and headstrong, Arians are straight-to-the-point and direct. Their desire to control often renders them jealous lovers. If they are given anything less than your undivided attention, they'll feel slighted.

As a lover, Aries has a strong, idealistic notion of romantic love—a view which must be respected by their partners lest the Ram's love flicker.

The Aries lover is faithful, needing to abide in his love so his highest romantic visions may be realized. Yet Aries is by nature flirtatious, and the Ram takes inordinate delight in winning friends and influencing people. Nothing encourages Aries as much as new dominion, especially over people. So it's not that they fall out of love when another attractive being walks into the picture; they just want to share their radiance.

The Aries symbol is a Ram's horns, seen by some as a fountain of youth, by others as idealistic leadership. At home in love, Aries lovers will go to great lengths for those they care for. Sacrifice comes easily to them, but is repeated only when duly recognized.

Actor Marlon Brando is a good Aries case in point. With his highly developed notions of romantic love, Brando, after many marriages, left Hollywood behind, finding refuge in the Pacific Islands with his Polynesian bride. What more romantic, ideal setting for love?

If you're an Aries, or love one, may the Ram be with you!

FAMOUS PEOPLE WITH SUN SIGN IN ARIES

Alan Arkin	Erica Jong
Johann Sebastian Bach	Ali McGraw
Warren Beatty	Steve McQueen
Marlon Brando	Gregory Peck
Joan Crawford	Diana Ross
Bette Davis	Omar Sharif
Doris Day	Simone Signoret
James Garner	Gloria Steinem
Billie Holiday	Spencer Tracy
Harry Houdini	Vincent van Gogh
Elton John	Tennessee Williams

TAURUS

April 21st through May 21st

Symbol: The Bull
Polarity: Female
Element: Earth
Quality: Fixed
Ruling Planet: Venus
Part of the Body Ruled: The neck and throat
Most Likable Trait: Dependability
Key Phrase: I HAVE
Lucky Day: Friday
Lucky Numbers: 4 and 6
Magical Birthstone: Emerald
Color: Pale blue and Mauve
Cities: Dublin, Lucerne, Leipzig, St. Louis
Countries: Ireland, Switzerland, Cyprus, Greece
Flowers: Violet and Poppy
Trees: Cypress and Apple
Metal: Copper
Animals Ruled: Cattle

This is the sign of the builder/producer, and in ancient times, the Taurus Bull was considered a fertility symbol. Unlike the fiery Aries, Taurus is earthy and sensual, the stabilizing force that can put the unchanneled energy of Aries to practical use. Taureans have a strong sense of home, and they're some of the most stable, solid lovers in the human spectrum.

With their sensuous, earthy orientation, Taureans tend to be artistic and creative, with a special bent toward creative crafts such as sculpture, pottery, and gardening. Since Taurus rules the throat, it is not surprising that many born under this sign are singers—some of the shower variety, and others, such as Barbra Streisand, Pete Seeger, and Stevie Wonder, of a much higher caliber.

The Taurus lover is loyal, doesn't fool around, and will expect the same faithfulness from others. Home is where their heart lies. They know a stable environment is essential to the sensuality they thrive on, and this causes the Bull to be most protective of love relationships. In romance, as in all other areas of their lives, they don't like change and are content to graze lazily on the field at hand, especially if the situation's tasty.

This sign's female polarity, combined with the ruling influence of Venus—the planet of love, pleasure, and the arts—serve to make Taurus a powerful, sensual lover. And Taurus cherishes its relationships with all the grounded, stable energy and attention one would expect of this fixed Earth sign. They worship security, and a stable home and love relationship are the foundations of that security. This generally easygoing lover is fun to be around, and reliable as earth, if stubborn at times.

The actor Henry Fonda was a classic Taurus—earthy and home-oriented, a man of few words. He was a bull-headed lover at the start, settling down after he fathered two children, Peter and Jane. On camera and off, Henry Fonda seemed a down-to-earth, conservative man—the strong silent type, the type who was generous but stubborn, tranquil but occasionally given to a wild temper. A Taurus type, in other words.

If you're a Taurus, or in love with one, get bullish on the Bull.

FAMOUS PEOPLE WITH SUN IN TAURUS

Ann-Margret
Fred Astaire
Richard Avedon
Burt Bacharach
Carol Burnett
Jill Clayburgh
Perry Como
Gary Cooper
Bing Crosby
Henry Fonda
Sigmund Freud
Martha Graham
Joseph Heller
Audrey Hepburn
Glenda Jackson
Reggie Jackson
Liberace
Rod McKuen
Shirley MacLaine
James Mason
Golda Meir
Jack Nicholson
Florence Nightingale
Ryan O'Neal
Al Pacino
Eva Peron
Tyrone Power
Sergei Prokofiev
Anthony Quinn
Bertrand Russell
William Shakespeare
Phil Silvers
James Stewart
Barbra Streisand
Shirley Temple
Rudolph Valentino
Leonardo da Vinci

GEMINI

May 22nd through June 21st

Symbol: The Twins
Polarity: Masculine
Element: Air
Quality: Mutable
Ruling Planet: Mercury
Part of the Body Ruled: Hands, arms, shoulders and lungs
Most Likable Trait: Responsiveness
Key Phrase: I THINK
Lucky Day: Wednesday
Lucky Numbers: 5 and 9
Magical Birthstone: Agate
Color: Yellow
Cities: London, San Francisco, Versailles, Melbourne
Countries: United States, Wales, Belgium
Flowers: Lily of the Valley and Lavender
Trees: Nut-bearing trees
Metal: Mercury
Animals Ruled: Brightly colored birds and butterflies

Gemini is the sign of the artist or inventor, a sign mercurial in nature, where high-speed thought is dominant. Gemini lovers have a nervous, quicksilver disposition. They tend to talk fast, promoting one idea after another in a never-ending stream. But don't look for constancy in their position, because the very idea is foreign to the Gemini state of being. More likely, the Twins will change their mind frequently and enthusiastically. This sign often experiences difficulty in coordinating thought and feeling, normally keeping these dimensions quite separate.

Because of their twin nature, Geminis are capable of handling many different things simultaneously—and this includes lovers. There are faithful Geminis to be sure, but even the most staid will exercise their roving imagination to the fullest. An air sign, it's not surprising that it's difficult to keep a grasp on Gemini. With their restless minds, the Twins are saturated with nervous energy and are constantly seeking new romantic horizons.

Geminis must have the freedom to be whomever they feel like being, whenever they want. If you happen to spend more than ten or fifteen minutes with a Gemini, you're likely to see the proof of Gemini's mutable quality, facing several different sides of their rapidly shifting nature. They're great fun most of the time and are sure to add spice to most any gathering. But you'll find it impossible to hold them to any standards but their own.

Geminis are characterized by an ageless appearance, as if somehow they're too busy to get old, and many find natives of this sign mighty attractive. "Exuberance," that's Gemini in a word, and that crackly eagerness keeps a youthful craving for joy and variety active. Geminis look young, act young, and keep things jumping.

Marilyn Monroe was a Gemini through and through—a different woman to every man who knew her. Every photograph of her portrayed a different facet of her personality. She seemed never to age, yet always to change. She was powerfully attractive, but no man could handle her.

If you're a Gemini, or find yourself irresistibly drawn to one, hold on to your hat . . . you're in for a ride!

FAMOUS PEOPLE WITH THE SUN IN GEMINI

Rachel Carson
Jacques Cousteau
Marquis de Sade
Arthur Conan Doyle
Bob Dylan
Clint Eastwood
Ralph Waldo Emerson
Douglas Fairbanks
Ian Fleming
Errol Flynn
Judy Garland
Paul Gauguin
Benny Goodman
Lillian Hellman
Xaviera Hollander
Bob Hope
Louis Jourdan
Pauline Kael
John F. Kennedy
Henry Kissinger
Paul McCartney
Dean Martin
Marilyn Monroe
Joe Namath
Joyce Carol Oates
Laurence Olivier
Cole Porter
Jean-Paul Sartre
Harriet Beecher Stowe
William Styron
Gene Wilder
Herman Wouk
Frank Lloyd Wright

CANCER

June 22nd through July 23rd

Symbol: The Crab
Polarity: Feminine
Element: Water
Quality: Cardinal
Ruling Planet: The Moon
Part of the Body Ruled: The breasts and stomach
Most Likable Trait: Loyalty
Key Phrase: I FEEL
Lucky Day: Monday
Lucky Numbers: 3 and 7
Magical Birthstone: Pearl
Color: Sea green and silver
Cities: Venice, Amsterdam, New York, Algiers
Countries: Scotland, Holland, New Zealand
Flowers: Larkspur and Acanthus
Trees: Trees rich in sap
Metal: Silver
Animals Ruled: Those with shell coverings

Ruled by the Moon and therefore by emotion, Cancers are an everchanging lot, their faces transforming like the lunar phases. This is the most highly charged sign of the zodiac, combining the fierce self-assertiveness of its cardinal quality with the fluid sensitivity and imagination of its water element.

Cancer is the sign of the prophet or teacher, and regardless of sex, the Crab possesses an unquenchable maternal instinct. Cancereans are lovers of humanity, and in their eyes we are all their little ones, in need of their nurturing. They are the eternal caretakers, treating all mankind as their kin.

While those born under this sign characteristically focus constant attention on the emotional lives of others, when it comes to their own feelings, Cancer operates in an extremely unassuming manner. Laughter will come out as a subtle chortle; anger emerges as a mild crabbiness. In the latter periods, which can sometimes turn into a blue funk, Cancers retreat into their crablike shells to hide out. For the outside world, the Crab's aim is to nourish their friends with physical and emotional foods of every dimension; for themselves, they aim to control emotion, their animator and occasional nemesis.

Cancereans are fun lovers to be around, as their humor is sophisticated and savvy in the ways of humankind. They love to laugh, and don't hesitate to laugh at themselves as well as others. The Crab is also a great provider, with a magic touch where money is concerned. Though they never feel completely secure themselves, Cancereans are always collecting things to protect the emotional stability and security of others. They practically revere the home—and the romance that goes with it—as a sanctuary. To be loved by a Cancer is to slip back to your mother's breast, being nursed by your creator. For some Cancereans, their mission may be the world; for others, no larger than the home. At whatever level, Cancereans care.

Meryl Streep is a Cancer, an Academy-Award-winning actress, and a devoted wife and mother. Somehow, this remarkable woman manages to do it all, lavishing intelligence and love on every one of her many roles. She is a highly charged and emotional woman who also possesses the cohesive presence of mind of a provider and caretaker. Meryl Streep lives with her family far away from the glitter of Hollywood in a Connecticut retreat nestled by a lake.

If you're a Cancer or are drawn to one of these nurturing souls, may the light of the Moon guide your shoreline walk.

FAMOUS PEOPLE WITH THE SUN IN CANCER

Alexander the Great	Mary McCarthy
Louis Armstrong	George McGovern
Polly Bergen	Bess Myerson
Ingmar Bergman	George Orwell
Bill Blass	Nelson Rockefeller
Yul Brynner	Ginger Rogers
James Cagney	Linda Ronstadt
Pierre Cardin	Carly Simon
Marc Chagall	Neil Simon
Oscar de la Renta	Isaac Bashevis Singer
Duke of Windsor	Barbara Stanwyck
Merv Griffin	Ringo Starr
Ernest Hemingway	Irving Stone
Judy Holliday	Donald Sutherland
Lena Horne	Henry David Thoreau
Franz Kafka	Abigail Van Buren
Helen Keller	E. B. White
Kris Kristofferson	Billy Wilder
Ann Landers	Andrew Wyeth

Leo

July 24th through August 23rd

Symbol: The Lion
Polarity: Masculine
Element: Fire
Quality: Fixed
Ruling Planet: The Sun
Part of the Body Ruled: The back, spine, and heart
Most Likable Trait: Exuberance
Key Phrase: I WILL
Lucky Day: Sunday
Lucky Numbers: 8 and 9
Magical Birthstone: Ruby
Colors: Gold and Orange
Cities: Rome, Prague, Damascus, Hollywood
Countries: France, Italy, Romania
Flowers: Sunflower and Marigold
Trees: All citrus trees
Metal: Gold
Animals Ruled: All felines

Ruled by the Sun, these radiant, sunny creatures are as playful as any lover in the zodiac. This is the sign of the king or president, and indeed Leo inevitably has a regal air. Symbolized by the lion, the king of the jungle, Leo is powerful and commanding, with a stately bearing. The Lion is a passionate soul, whose attention, more often than not, is centered on himself or herself. Flattery is like catnip, scorn like a claw across the face. The Leo Lion needs to shine, and usually has no difficulty attracting the attention of others.

Traditionally, those born into this sign make great performers and actors. At center stage, they are indisputably in the limelight, where they can do their own thing, in their own way. And in romance, their behavior is no different. Leo will play second fiddle to none, demanding the undivided attention and affection of his mate. From start to finish, Leo will settle for nothing less than majesty and glory in relationships. "Starring Leo" is the way the billing over the bedroom door should read. And after basking in all your applause, Leo will return the favor by gently purring.

Leo is sexy, fun, and full of life. The Lion is a passionate lover, fired up with emotion and ambition. But the Leo lust for attention will forever impart to this sign a roving eye. The Lion may very well remain true to the core, absolutely faithful. But given a chance encounter with a new, dashing admirer, Leo will flirt as much as possible without undressing.

Consider Gracie Allen and Lucille Ball, both solid Leos. These two vivacious women have ridden their ambitions to the glittering heights, turning their good humor and need for attention into stellar careers as comediennes. With their charismatic, humorous personalities, they've touched many people and were given great power in return. Each was also very happily, and publicly, married to her TV co-star. And each of their classic series played off their Leonine traits, joking at their self-importance.

Whether you're a Leo or are blessed to be in a relationship with one, may you bask in the bright Leo sunshine.

FAMOUS PEOPLE WITH THE SUN IN LEO

Bella Abzug
Gracie Allen
Lucille Ball
Tony Bennett
Napoleon Bonaparte
Ray Bradbury
Fidel Castro
Coco Chanel
Julia Child
Robert De Niro
Mike Douglas
Alexandre Dumas
Amelia Earhart
Mata Hari
Alfred Hitchcock
Dustin Hoffman
John Huston
Mick Jagger
Herman Melville
Benito Mussolini
Annie Oakley
Carroll O'Connor
Jacqueline Kennedy Onassis
Peter O'Toole
Dorothy Parker
Roman Polanski
Robert Redford
Haile Selassie
Yves Saint Laurent
George Bernard Shaw
Leon Uris
Mae West
Shelley Winters
Orville Wright

VIRGO

August 24th through September 23rd

Symbol: The Virgin
Polarity: Feminine
Element: Earth
Quality: Mutable
Ruling Planet: Mercury
Part of the Body Ruled: The nervous system and the intestines
Most Likable Trait: Conscientiousness
Key Phrase: I ANALYZE
Lucky Day: Wednesday
Lucky Numbers: 3 and 5
Magical Birthstone: Sapphire
Colors: Navy Blue and Gray
Cities: Paris, Boston, Heidelberg, Strasbourg
Countries: Turkey, Greece, West Indies
Flowers: Morning Glory and Pansy
Trees: Nut-bearing trees
Metal: Mercury
Animals Ruled: Small domestic pets

Virgo is the sign for holy hermits, and many of those born into it are loners. It is also the sign of the craftsman or critic, and the keen Virgo eye is quick to note flaws in everything and everyone, self included. Virgo is supercritical and obsessed with perfection, traits that are sometimes problematic, sometimes helpful.

An Earth sign, ruled by the action-oriented Mercury, Virgo keeps a constant eye toward improvement and is a real *doer*, spending time and energy at useful tasks. But unlike their attention-grabbing Leo neighbors, Virgo does not wait for recognition. There's never any time for the awards ceremony, for Virgo's already caught up in his next bit of work. But these industrious workers tend to take on more than they can handle. In this manner, they stress a system that's already charged with Mercury's tension. While not brimming with nervous energy, the way Gemini is, beneath Virgo's quiet, reserved manner there's a dynamo whirring at a million rpm's.

Not being social by nature, and feeling uneasy in crowds, Virgos are not exactly party animals, but they can be great fun. They are among the best mimics in the zodiac—sharing honors with Gemini—producing the likes of Peter Sellers and Sid Caesar. Despite their eccentricities, though, natives of this sign are generally ultraneat and exacting in all dimensions of their life.

So it goes with the Virgo lover—chaste, highly discriminating, discreet, prudent. Virgo loves true romance, but if you tinge the relationship with gushy sentiment or vulgarity, they'll be gone before you have time to voice your apology. These straight shooters demand the truth plain and simple. For them, sensuality is second in love; first comes the responsibility of the relationship. They are not needy for love, wanting it but knowing they're fine without it. So they do not rush into affairs. They cannot be pushed, pressed, or pursued in romance. Rather, Virgos must be met, punctually, with clarity and wit.

Lauren Bacall, Ingrid Bergman, and Sophia Loren are all Virgos. Each embodies the cool-power of Virgo love, each demands as much from the world as from herself, each has used her perfectionism to chart a unique course. In lives filled with cinematic and real romance, these three women all act out the fullest expression of the Virgin as Earth mother.

If you were born a Virgo or happen to love one, give thanks, take the criticism with a grain of salt, and keep it simple.

FAMOUS PEOPLE WITH THE SUN IN VIRGO

Lauren Bacall	Bret Harte
Anne Bancroft	Samuel Johnson
Ingrid Bergman	Jesse James
Leonard Bernstein	Elia Kazan
Jacqueline Bisset	Gene Kelly
Sid Caesar	D. H. Lawrence
Agatha Christie	Sophia Loren
Craig Claiborne	Rocky Marciano
Sean Connery	Jessica Mitford
Jimmy Connors	Bob Newhart
Jackie Cooper	Arnold Palmer
Queen Elizabeth I	Leo Tolstoi
Greta Garbo	Lily Tomlin
Ben Gazzara	Racquel Welch
Buddy Hackett	H. G. Wells

LIBRA

September 24th through October 23rd

Symbol: The Scales
Polarity: Masculine
Element: Air
Quality: Cardinal
Ruling Planet: Venus
Part of the Body Ruled: The lower back, buttocks, and kidneys
Most Likable Trait: Charm
Key Phrase: I BALANCE
Lucky Day: Friday
Lucky Numbers: 6 and 9
Magical Birthstone: Opal
Colors: Blue and Lavender
Cities: Vienna, Copenhagen, Charleston, Lisbon
Countries: Burma, China, Tibet, Argentina, Japan
Flowers: Rose, Cosmos, and Hydrangea
Trees: Almond, Cypress, and Ash
Metal: Copper
Animals Ruled: Snakes and lizards

Life is a balancing act for Libra, and though others might use emotion or intuition to weigh the many different aspects and pieces in the puzzle of life, Librans use intellect. For this reason alone, though ruled by the emotive Venus, Librans are often unaware of some of the emotional subtleties that inevitably exist in relationships.

Some say that Libra is indecisive. But those born under this sign would counter that they're merely being careful, logical, and reasonable about the conclusions they reach. In any case, they are truth-seekers who welcome opinions and viewpoints that challenge their own. Librans relish a good argument.

With their preoccupying concern for balancing two sides, it is not surprising that the concept of partnership is fundamental to Libra. Ruled by Venus, Librans tend to exhibit a softness and a sensuality that balances their rational side. Many Librans are beautiful, and all are likely to have fashioned lovely living environments. Love is an essential, no matter how intellectually a Libran might view it, and the influence of the Scales make these people sophisticated lovers.

A strain of fickleness runs throughout this air sign, rendering Librans as vulnerable as their partners. To sway in the balance is the state of being for this sign, and although occasionally one might come to a rest at equilibrium, it is usually only momentarily. Still, since Librans place great importance on establishing harmony, interpersonal diplomacy is practiced to keep affairs in balance. Librans are kind and fair people who are loving and beloved.

Libra is the sign of the statesman or manager. Mahatma Ghandi was a Libra, for instance, as was Dwight D. Eisenhower. And we can see loving diplomacy at its highest state of development in both of these people. In the marital lives of these men, both gave their charm freely, creating balanced families. Both acknowledged interest in women besides their wives, but only apparently to set the scales swinging.

Alert, affectionate, sympathetic, the Libran embodies some of the best features of any lover. On balance, you're lucky if you are one, or love one. . . .

FAMOUS PEOPLE WITH THE SUN IN LIBRA

Julie Andrews
Brigitte Bardot
David Ben-Gurion
Lenny Bruce
Art Buchwald
Truman Capote
Ray Charles
e. e. cummings
Catherine Deneuve
Dwight D. Eisenhower
T. S. Eliot
William Faulkner
F. Scott Fitzgerald
Mohandas K. Ghandi
George Gershwin
Rita Hayworth
Charlton Heston
Buster Keaton
John Lennon
Mickey Mantle
Groucho Marx
Marcello Mastroianni
Arthur Miller
Yves Montand
Roger Moore
Luciano Pavarotti
Juan Peron
Rex Reed
Mickey Rooney
Eleanor Roosevelt
Ed Sullivan
Gore Vidal
Barbara Walters
Oscar Wilde

SCORPIO

October 24th through November 22nd

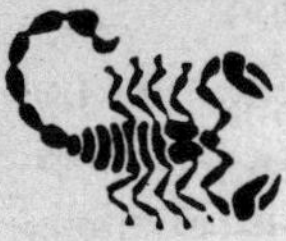

Symbol: The Scorpion
Polarity: Feminine
Element: Water
Quality: Fixed
Ruling Planet: Pluto and Mars
Part of the Body Ruled: The genitals
Most Likable Trait: Idealism
Key Phrase: I DESIRE
Lucky Day: Tuesday
Lucky Numbers: 2 and 4
Magical Birthstone: Topaz
Colors: Crimson, Burgundy, and Maroon
Cities: Liverpool; New Orleans; Washington, D.C.; Newcastle
Countries: Norway, Algeria, Morocco, Tahiti
Flowers: Chrysanthemum and Rhododendron
Trees: Blackthorn and bushy trees
Metal: Plutonium
Animals Ruled: Insects and crustaceans

No sign has a livelier reputation than Scorpio, and rightly so. For Scorpios are intense, passionate lovers, willing to die for their love if need be. Under the influence of Pluto, all their actions are infused with an obsessive quality, and because of this they live in a world of their own. The sign of the governor or inspector, Scorpio is known to have high standards in general, although they apply those standards to areas of interest peculiar to them.

They typically seek out the secrets of life and death, and many of those born under this sign become doctors or healers.

Scorpios are calm on the surface, raging below. It's not rage at anyone or anything, it's just the influence of Mars, which stirs them constantly. When they're in love, it's head over heels, and little can keep them from it. Their loyalty is strong, their passion sometimes overwhelming. Sex is of great interest to these natives—not surprisingly, since Scorpio rules the genitals—and their desire for sensual exploration often outstrips that of their partners. Scorpio makes a powerful, fearless lover, who's not afraid of excess when it comes to drink, drugs, and romance.

But while this rather secretive sign is filled with desire, like the animal itself, Scorpio is liable to sting when upset. They are quick to fall madly in love, but if you try to change Scorpio, or get him to conform to your worldview rather than going along with his, you'll probably get bitten. They love and live their own way, striving quietly to overcome all of life's darker dimensions.

Since Scorpio is concerned with transcendence, it's not surprising that some Scorpios take a higher path, sublimating their passions into purer forms. This is the case with Billy Graham. Others transform their obsession into fairy-tale lives, as was the case with Grace Kelly. Most deal with the mysteries of existence on a daily basis, and this infuses them with a magnetism. Scorpio men are hypnotic, Scorpio women are the most renowned *femme fatales* of the zodiac.

In its evolved form, the Scorpion is transformed into a soaring eagle, above all life. Scorpions and their lovers, take flight!

FAMOUS PEOPLE WITH THE SUN IN SCORPIO

Marie Antoinette
Charles Bronson
Richard Burton
Albert Camus
Johnny Carson
Dick Cavett
Prince Charles of England
Walter Cronkite
Marie Curie
Indira Gandhi
Billy Graham
Katharine Hepburn
Rock Hudson
Grace Kelly
Robert Kennedy
Vivien Leigh
Martin Luther
Charles Manson
Claude Monet
Georgia O'Keeffe
George Patton
Pablo Picasso
Sylvia Plath
Emily Post
Will Rogers
Theodore Roosevelt
Jonas Salk
Robert Louis Stevenson
Joan Sutherland
Dylan Thomas
Voltaire
Kurt Vonnegut

SAGITTARIUS

November 23rd through December 21st

Symbol: The Archer
Polarity: Masculine
Element: Fire
Quality: Mutual
Ruling Planet: Jupiter
Part of the Body Ruled: The liver, hips, and thighs
Most Likable Trait: Optimism
Key Phrase: I SEE
Lucky Day: Thursday
Lucky Numbers: 5 and 7
Magical Birthstone: Turquoise
Color: Purple
Cities: Budapest, Cologne, Toledo, Acapulco
Countries: Spain, Hungary, Australia
Flowers: Narcissus, Holly, and Dandelion
Trees: Mulberry, Oak, and Birch
Metal: Tin
Animals Ruled: Horse

This is the sign of the archer, a centaur—half man/half horse—who fires arrows to some higher aim. The aim of this sign is primarily to unite the bestial half with the human side, and in that quest, Sagittarians travel as fast and as furious as their arrows. The journey itself becomes of primary importance to Sagittarius, and no other sign has such psychic and physical wanderlust. Ever optimistic, Sagittarius is firmly convinced that life right now is as good as it's ever been, and that the best is still to come.

Sagittarians are guileless lovers, without a mean bone in their bodies. Yet, with surprising frequency, they'll hurt you with their candid, tactless assessments of your life, all in the name of truth and friendship. They can't lie—it's not in their makeup—so what they tell you usually is exactly what they think. If you can roll with their inadvertent punches, however, Sagittarius is the life of the party, a driving wit that just won't quit.

Known as the sign of the sage or counselor, Sagittarians make great teachers, especially of science, philosophy, and religion. Many performers also share this sign, fortified by their love of fun and the Sagittarian refusal to take life too seriously. Should disaster strike, Sagittarius is eminently capable of taking it in stride; for to them it's only a moment in their journey, a speck on the lifelong flight of their arrow. They're here to teach, surely, but Sagittarians are also quite adept at learning, and seek intellectual and spiritual illumination by anyone and everyone they meet.

The mutable quality of Sagittarius exaggerates their already strong wandering streak, making this sign much more prone to small flames of flirtation than long-term serious relationships. When they *do* get fired up, whether it's for a day, a week, or a year, the Sagittarius lover nears meltdown. Either way, these freedom-loving, generous centaurs attract many lovers, and it's only Sagittarian's lack of idealism that keeps their romantic lives manageable. Lovers are seen for who they are, in the context of all people.

Jane Fonda is a Sagittarian, a fiery, mutable, male-polarized woman of action. As might be expected, apart from being an excellent performer, she's also an aerobics teacher. An outspoken woman, she refuses to silence herself when she's taking a controversial position, and her actions indicate her view of life as a journey, with many stops to come. Woody Allen is also a Sagittarian, and in his life we can clearly see a man of wit, who refuses to get caught up in the seriousness of it all. Through his writing and acting we are given a teaching of wisdom disguised as foolishness. Both these superstar Sagittarians have attracted many lovers, and each has sorted through, selecting a mate.

If you're an archer, or find yourself quivering near one, bon voyage!

FAMOUS PEOPLE WITH THE SUN IN SAGITTARIUS

Woody Allen
Jane Austen
Ludwig van Beethoven
Leonid Brezhnev
William F. Buckley
Maria Callas
Dale Carnegie
Winston Churchill
Sammy Davis, Jr.
Charles de Gaulle
Joe DiMaggio
Walt Disney
Kirk Douglas
Chris Evert Lloyd
Douglas Fairbanks, Jr.
Jane Fonda
Boris Karloff
Harpo Marx
Margaret Mead
Bette Midler
Lee Remick
Frank Sinatra
James Thurber
Mark Twain
Liv Ullmann
Dick Van Dyke
Flip Wilson

CAPRICORN

December 22nd through January 20th

Symbol: The Goat
Polarity: Feminine
Element: Earth
Quality: Cardinal
Ruling Planet: Saturn
Part of the Body Ruled: The bones, joints, and knees
Most Likable Trait: Steadiness
Key Phrase: I USE
Lucky Day: Saturday
Lucky Numbers: 2 and 8
Magical Birthstone: Garnet
Colors: Dark Green and Brown
Cities: Oxford, Boston, Brussels, Chicago, Montreal
Countries: Mexico, Afghanistan, Bulgaria, India
Flowers: Carnation and Ivy
Trees: Pine, Elm, and Poplar
Metal: Lead
Animals Ruled: Goats and animals with cloven hoofs

Like Sagittarius, Capricorn is represented by a composite creature, a mythical Goat with the tail of a fish. The dominant and most visible characteristics of this sign are represented by the goat—a determined climber, a practical, serious, and cautious animal. There may be some slow, rocky going at the start of any project Capricorn tackles, but as the Goat gets the feel of things, it gets stronger and the task grows lighter. Capricorn is likely to succeed in the material arena, accumulating substantial wealth and power.

As to the fish tail, the Goat would prefer not to deal with it. The tail's water-based orientation feels quite foreign to the Capricorn, whose element is Earth. This watery side to Capricorn is embodied in this sign's powerful unexpressed emotion.

Capricorns revere the past and the wisdom of old age, and are fascinated with the secret of eternal youth, finding life progressively easier, happier, and more fulfilling with the unfurling of each successive phase of their existence. They'll outstrip even Gemini in the race to stay young, discovering more and more of life's little secrets as they go.

Those born under this earthy sign tend to be conservative lovers. Rather than forge new boundaries and explore uncharted waters, Capricorn is filled with respect for those who've already smoothed the path upward. Tradition is held high, and though some would call this snobby, to the Goat it's a matter of practicality. Capricorn reveres the success of others almost as much as its own.

These social butterflies always mix in the right circles and dress appropriately for any occasion. They are exceptionally organized—some would say regimented—and only when their life is operating on schedule can the Capricorn relax. Only when their vast need for material security is close to being satisfied does Capricorn become warm and affectionate. Then the calculating, opportunistic creature fades, revealing one of great wisdom, loyalty, and love.

Benjamin Franklin was a classic Capricorn, an ambitious, persevering, diplomatic, and reserved social climber. Like the Goat, he could digest anything and get nourishment from it. He climbed socially, politically, and scientifically via his kite, and romantically via his many reported liaisons while serving in France. This hardworking, determined climber may have written *Poor Richard's*, but he ended up living the *Lifestyle of the Rich and Famous*.

Capricorns and their admirers, may the underlying emotions wash gently upon your shore while you ascend the mountain's heights.

FAMOUS PEOPLE WITH THE SUN IN CAPRICORN

Charles Addams	Danny Kaye
Muhammad Ali	Martin Luther King, Jr.
Steve Allen	Rudyard Kipling
Isaac Asimov	Jack London
Joan Baez	Mao Tse-tung
Humphrey Bogart	Henri Matisse
Al Capone	Henry Miller
Paul Cezanne	Sir Isaac Newton
Anton Chekhov	Richard M. Nixon
Marlene Dietrich	Edgar Allan Poe
Faye Dunaway	Elvis Presley
Benjamin Franklin	Paul Revere
Cary Grant	Anwar Sadat
J. Edgar Hoover	Albert Schweitzer
Howard Hughes	Joseph Stalin
Joan of Arc	J. R. R. Tolkien

aquarius

January 21st through February 19th

Symbol: The Water Bearer
Polarity: Masculine
Element: Air
Quality: Fixed
Ruling Planet: Uranus and Saturn
Part of the Body Ruled: The circulatory system, shins, and ankles
Most Likable Trait: Friendliness
Key Phrase: I KNOW
Lucky Day: Wednesday
Lucky Numbers: 1 and 7
Magical Birthstone: Amethyst
Color: Bright Blue
Cities: Stockholm, Moscow, Buenos Aires, Salzburg
Countries: Russia, Sweden, Ethiopia
Flowers: Orchid
Trees: Fruit trees
Metal: Uranium
Animals Ruled: Large birds

The ever-curious Aquarius is considered the sign of the truth seeker or scientist. This is the sign of the future, and many postulate that as Aquarius thinks, so will the world think in fifty years. There is contradiction inherent in this sign, however, ruled as it is by two planets with nearly opposing influences. The Uranian side demands moment-to-moment freedom, especially of ideas, while the side ruled by Saturn demands that stability reign. The result is a highly original if eccentric character, difficult enough for the Aquarian himself to pin down, and just about impossible for the other signs of the zodiac to grasp.

As the Water Bearer, Aquarius is depicted pouring water out of a huge container, sharing its abundance of new ideas. Newness is an integral part of the Aquarian character, and in dress, behavior, and art, the Water Bearer is likely to be a leader of the avant-garde. Of all the genius celebrated in the Hall of Fame, the vast majority of the most renowned innovators were born under the sign of Aquarius.

Aquarians are typically simple, sincere people who are enormously popular and who place great value on friendship. But despite the great number of friendly relationships this sign establishes so easily, deeper affairs are often awkwardly managed and curiously short-lived. The characteristic exploratory tinkering is part of the Aquarian genius, and in relationships this sometimes includes moving from friend to friend, and lover to lover, in quest of a deeper truth. In fact, the ever-curious Aquarius is considered the sign of the truth seeker or scientist.

Aquarians may have a rather cool way of relating to others in romance. They are stubborn and full of surprises. Because they're ruled by two such different planets, Aquarians have an uncertain sense of self, causing them to hesitate before entering into deep relationships. When they do, however, they are likely to be faithful and trusting, as any form of dishonesty goes against the Aquarius grain.

Paul Newman is an Aquarian, a performer/director/race-car driver who projects an image of detached friendliness, who seems always to be in quest of real truth. Newman chose a very strong mate, actress Joanne Woodward, and has stuck by her for decades, despite any differences they may have had. Even Cool Hand Luke has his warm side.

Seekers of truth, bearers of the fountain of ideas, sons and daughters of Aquarius, and those drawn to their dreams, may your present smooth the way to a more perfect future.

FAMOUS PEOPLE WITH THE SUN IN AQUARIUS

Susan B. Anthony	Douglas MacArthur
Mikhail Baryshnikov	Norman Mailer
Jack Benny	Wolfgang Amadeus Mozart
Aaron Burr	Paul Newman
Edie Cantor	Jackson Pollock
Lewis Carroll	Ronald Reagan
Charles Darwin	Vanessa Redgrave
Charles Dickens	Burt Reynolds
Christian Dior	Jackie Robinson
Thomas Alva Edison	Norman Rockwell
Federico Fellini	Franklin Delano Roosevelt
W. C. Fields	Telly Savalas
Clark Gable	Franz Schubert
Zane Grey	Jules Verne
James Joyce	Virginia Woolf
Abraham Lincoln	
Charles Lindberg	

PISCES

February 20th through March 20th

Symbol: Two fishes tied to each other and swimming in opposite directions
Polarity: Feminine
Element: Water
Quality: Mutable
Ruling Planets: Jupiter and Neptune
Part of the Body Ruled: The feet
Most Likable Trait: Compassion
Key Phrase: I BELIEVE
Lucky Day: Friday
Lucky Numbers: 2 and 6
Magical Birthstone: Aquamarine
Colors: Pale Green and Turquoise
Cities: Casablanca, Alexandria, Lisbon, Seville, Dublin
Countries: Portugal, the Sahara Desert
Flowers: Water Lily, White Poppy, Jonquil
Trees: Fig and Willow
Metal: Platinum
Animals Ruled: Fish

The last sign in the zodiac, Pisces, like neighboring Aquarius, is ruled by two planets. Jupiter rules religion, while Neptune rules mysticism: Under their combined influence most Pisceans are otherworldly, dreamy, and spiritual. They make for extraordinarily sensitive lovers, who embody much of the wisdom from all the signs that have come before. Pisceans are also gentle, easygoing, and quite charming. You see, they've had time to ripen and integrate the good and the bad of all other astrological signs.

Pisceans are imaginative, perceptive lovers, extremely attractive to most, truly compatible with few. They are ruled by the sign of the poet or interpreter, the sign of true love, faith, and tranquility. At the end of the astrological spectrum, they've seen it all. Emotional and vulnerable, Pisces does not possess the protective shell of the other two water signs, Cancer and Scorpio. Lacking this armor, Pisceans often hide their real feelings, in effect acting offstage. And though they tend to be shy, many of them are drawn to the theater, performing brilliantly with their innate, intuitive acting abilities. Some turn to politics, still others to religion. In both arenas, they manage to combine spectacular performance with a higher intuition.

Pisceans contain a wellspring of pity and care for the sick and the weak. Utterly nonjudgmental, they are quick to help whomever, wherever, and whenever they can. For example, when he heard of the incredible suffering in Bangladesh, George Harrison rearranged his life, organizing a multimillion-dollar concert benefit. And when she was touched by the deaths of many AIDS victims, Elizabeth Taylor organized a series of benefits, raising millions and confronting the tragedy head-on. Both these superstar performers have a warm, dreamy quality to them. Both have enjoyed lives rich with romance.

Swimmers of Pisces, and those who join them, may your otherworldly intuitions enrich your love live, and enlighten us all.

FAMOUS PEOPLE WITH THE SUN IN PISCES

Harry Belafonte
Alexander Graham Bell
Michael Caine
Frederic Chopin
Nicolaus Copernicus
Cyrano de Bergerac
Wyatt Earp
Albert Einstein
Galileo Galilei
Jackie Gleason
Jean Harlow
Oliver Wendell Holmes
Edward M. Kennedy
Jack Kerouac
Lee Marvin
Edna St. Vincent Millay
Glenn Miller
Liza Minnelli
Ralph Nader
Anais Nin
Sydney Poitier
Elizabeth Taylor
John Updike
Gloria Vanderbilt
George Washington

CHAPTER III

SIGN COMPATIBILITY—THE ELUSIVE MATCHED PAIR

Now that you've gained an understanding of the general character and personality of each individual astrological sign, it's time to take a look to the stars in love! There are seventy-eight different combinations of Sun signs, seventy-eight fascinating romantic possibilities, each with its own particular attractions and harmonies, strengths and weaknesses, frustrations and difficulties. And of these seventy-eight romantic possibilities, twelve unique combinations are possible for each and every one of us.

Sun-sign compatibility study will provide the astrological know-how you need to more fully understand the people you meet and how you are likely to interact with them. In a few brief statements, such compatibility comparison can capture the essence of a magical meeting.

A complete study of Sun-sign compatibility would start with the two signs' relative positions in the zodiac. Are they adjacent signs? Opposite signs? Separated by two or three or four other signs? These relative positions have a significance that holds true for any two Sun signs, and from this many of the relationship's basic tensions and assets can be understood.

You would then consider the qualities, polarities, and elements of the signs you're interested in, noting how they are mixed.

And finally, you would study the individual character traits that make up each sign, searching for similarities and differences. If one partner is very private, a Pisces, for instance, and the other a more public character, such as a Leo, there's a problematic tension right at the start. Furthermore, Pisces is a water sign and Leo is a fire sign, perhaps the two least mixable elements. Still, such relationships can, and do, work. In many cases, the Leo partner might be showing off enough for the two of them, while Pisces provides the perfect audience.

The first level of comparison is between your element natures. People whose signs share the same element are often powerfully attracted, and many of these relationships become close. But for some, even of the same element, this very similarity breeds a lack of excitement or a reinforcement of shared weakness. No sign is categorically perfect or disastrous for any other, and each combination offers certain strong possibilities together with opportunities for failure.

Here, then, are suggestions on how the signs' element natures mix with each other:

* * *

Fire with Fire: When a fire sign meets another fire sign, there's bound to be heat. Tremendous enthusiasm and passion can be expected from such a match, but little compromise.

Fire with Earth: Fire and earth often get along quite well; the fire sign provides energy and animation, while the earth sign gives the relationship stability and security. But frustration may arise in earth over fire's impulsive qualities, and in fire over earth's complacency.

Fire with Air: Fire and air make for a truly exciting combination, the intellect of the air sign sparking lively with fire's enthusiasm. Problems may arise, however, when the air sign fails to express his or her feelings, or when the fire sign is lax in taking care of day-to-day details.

Fire with Water: These two elements would seem an unlikely pair. And, in fact, water signs tend to find fire signs insensitive, while fire feels its energy dampened by water's fluid sensitivity. They rarely make it to the altar. These elements do much better as friends than as lovers.

Earth with Earth: When earth meets earth, they're bound to form a solid, grounded pair, building from foundation first. With so much sedate stability, however, earth signs may have a tendency to turn each other to stone, or never raise themselves above ground level.

Earth with Air: Earth and air often mix well together. Earth tends to become less weighty and dense under the influence of air's ideas, while air becomes more steady from earth's practical skills. Together, however, this combination is unlikely to go deep or far.

Earth with Water: Earth and water admire much about each other, and for good reason. Water is touched by earth's skill, and earth fascinated by water's sensitivity. In a committed relationship, however, earth can become frustrated with water's diluted practicality, and water can be left unimpressed by earth's insistence on order.

Air with Air: This is a lively combination, each air sign wafting higher than the other on their lofty currents of communication. In their airy flight, though, deeper feelings may sometimes get overlooked.

Air with Water: Air and water do nicely together, blending air's tendency toward thought with water's intuition to produce a shared higher state. But when this pair really gets going, they can occasionally become too imaginative for their own good.

Water with Water: When water meets water it's hardly surprising that ecstatic tears of joyous, dreamy romance result. But because of the sensitive, intuitive nature of this element, when troubles arise, they may remain waterlogged, finding it hard to pull themselves out of difficult situations.

Beyond element compatibility, there is Sun-sign compatibility. Here again, every combination has its positive potential—*and* its possible pitfalls. Here is a chart inscribed with the signs of the zodiac. Find the two signs you're interested in, then check the key below to find out how such signs are likely to fare in love.

sun-sign compatibility

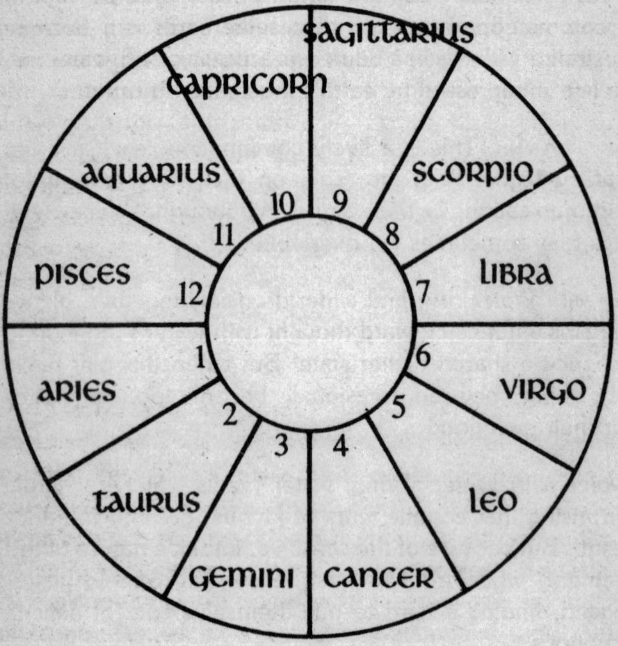

Prospects for love if the Sun signs are:

The same (such as Leo-Leo, or Gemini-Gemini): Like-minded souls are apt to greatly admire each other, enjoying a deep, instant rapport. But committed love relationships inevitably require compromise, and perhaps the least equipped pair for such settlements is a same-sign couple. Though like Sun signs are powerfully attracted to each other, seeing their glory reflected in another, they can also easily cancel each other out with their similar weaknesses. Consider a couple both born under the sign of Cancer. Cancer loves to nurture others, give them tasty things to eat, and make them feel good. These are lovely qualities—ones that any human would be better off for having. But if two people mother each other incessantly, there is great likelihood they'll both end up a couple of couch potatoes.

Adjacent (such as Aries-Taurus, or Sagittarius-Capricorn): Couples with adjacent Sun signs are frequently well-mated. Although these signs will always have opposite polarities and different ruling elements, the radical differences between the two often provide stimulating satisfaction. Moreover, the strengths of one sign often balance the weaknesses of the other. But occasionally these two signs become preoccupied with the differences between them, and this may prevent a relationship from being long-lasting.

Alternate (such as Cancer-Virgo, or Leo-Libra): These combinations often make excellent matches, balanced and without great tensions. Expect a terrific time, but don't count on commitment.

In the same quality (cardinal, fixed, or mutable; signs with two others between them, such as Pisces-Gemini, or Scorpio-Aquarius): Because these signs have both different polarity and a different element, couples who share the same quality are still likely to be made up of very different people. Although same-quality signs are frequently fascinated by their other differences—and may even form lasting, loving relationships—they sometimes end up riding their differences off in separate directions.

In the same element (fire, air, earth, or water; signs with three others between them, such as Aries-Leo, or Libra-Aquarius): This is a stellar astrological combination, where both lovers are quite similar in nature. But while they are able to give each other strong support and understanding, emphasizing their strong points, they must also keep an eye out for shared weaknesses that both might choose not to recognize.

In Quincunx (signs with four others between them, such as Taurus-Sagittarius, or Libra-Pisces): Signs in quincunx differ not only in quality and in their ruling element, but in polarity as well. For this reason, the differences between these signs are often difficult to overcome. Don't rule out the possibility of romance for this pair, however. Two very different folks can be quite capable of admiring each other's strokes.

Opposite (signs directly across the chart, with five signs on either side of them, such as Aries-Libra, or Virgo-Pisces): This is a much-favored duo, with great intimacy and a strong sense of balance. Even with these strengths assured, however, differences may set in. These couples are supremely balanced naturally, each almost exactly compensating for the other's weaknesses, each adding that magic ingredient that had otherwise been lacking. In each of these Sun-sign combinations, the pairs complement each other, fitting together like parts of a jigsaw puzzle. But even with a perfect fit, the parts can get misaligned, and differences accentuated.

Any romantic relationship can work if there is sufficient love. But being aware of your lover's astrological makeup will make it easier to foresee the trouble spots and make allowances for the differences between the two of you. And don't forget that many factors—especially your rising signs—can influence your or your lover's personality. Just as no one sign is guaranteed to be perfect for another, neither is it impossible for two people born under seemingly incompatible Sun signs to find love and long-lasting happiness. The following match-ups provide an idea of both the strengths and weaknesses of every astrological combination:

Aries-Aries: This dynamic duo is twice charged by the fiery energy of Mars, doubly idealistic and original. Dashing and enterprising, this couple is often given to impulse. Yet because each partner tends to be vulnerable and impatient, momentary friction can lead to a prolonged clashing of these hotheads. The typical Aries take-charge energy and the desire to dominate can lead to fierce competition between two Rams, sometimes taking a heavy toll on their initial passionate link and intuitive harmony. But if each can find their own, nonconflicting projects to concentrate on, the Aries's competitive nature doesn't have to be destructive to this pair.

Aries-Taurus: There is a strong mutual fascination between these two signs, whose differences seem to complement and balance each other so extraordinarily. Fiery Aries provides the relationship with enthusiasm and initiative, while Taurus lends stability and sensuality. There are bound to be rough times, however. Aries's constant need to reaffirm his individuality and search for new experiences grates on the possessive, jealous side of the earthy Bull, who's invariably set in his ways. But the mutual attraction of these two signs can be long-lasting. Over time, Aries will often grow to appreciate the grounded dependability of Taurus, while the Bull need not feel rejected by the impulsive nature of the Ram, reminding himself that it's simply a part of Aries's fiery nature.

Aries-Gemini: The prognosis for this lively pair is most definitely good, since both signs share a desire to discover and explore new ground. The unflagging enthusiasm of Aries fans the spark of Gemini's intellect, and together these two create concepts new to them both. While Aries will likely be the decision-maker of this pair, versatile Gemini will delight in the challenge of continually sparking the Ram's interest. Since both signs are prone to change, their constantly changing relationship will very likely wind through quite a few twists and turns. They do need to pay careful attention to the strong subcurrent of their emotions, however, something easily overlooked in the fire of their quick thinking.

Aries-Cancer: As a romantic proposition, this pair is an iffy bet, though they often make fabulous friends. Initially, the Ram and the Crab may be completely enamored of each other, the self-assertiveness typical of their shared cardinal quality adding to their sexual attraction. But due to their temperamental differences, in deeper relationships difficulties frequently set in. The cautious, emotional Cancer is often saddened or hurt by Aries's aggressiveness and seeming insensitivity. The adventuresome Aries is constantly perplexed by Cancer's supersensitive outlook, and feels hemmed in by Cancer's love of security and domesticity. In the end, both signs would do well to look for a way out.

Aries-Leo: This combination of fire signs usually burns brightly. With Aries so proud to lead off the zodiac, and Leo basking under the sunny admiration of his many followers, these two form a radiant pair. Brilliant individually, brimming with enthusiasm, they share an unquenchable appetite for exploration—in the bedroom as well as in other areas of their lives. Both are leaders, with a tendency to dominate. To keep from clashing over who should be at center stage, they must cultivate patience and self-control. If they can learn to compromise, and control their egos from time to time, a glorious future is in store for this couple.

Aries-Virgo: In this mutually beneficial arrangement, Aries may gain from Virgo's thoughtful practicality, while Virgo becomes energized by the powerful initiative of Aries. There are differences, to be sure, but in the best of all worlds this match will survive intact. Aries is the leader, the adventurer, and in perfect support Virgo keeps pace. Aries is the conceiver of ideas; Virgo brings them forth. However, if these two fail to appreciate their different characters, their relationship may never really get off the ground. Virgo may be critical of Aries's wild ways, while

Aries is too impatient to try to uncover the enigmatic, intellectual side of Virgo.

Aries - Libra: When these two signs join together, they're living proof that opposites do attract. Theirs is a deeply connected partnership, with each sign almost precisely compensating for the weaknesses of the other, each providing the magic missing ingredient that makes it all work. Libra gives balance to Aries's explosive power, while Aries's aggressiveness kindles Libra's sensual enthusiasm. But as they grow together, both signs must guard against focusing negatively on their differences, which are the very qualities that balance their relationship. Because once Libra's search for harmony begins to clash with the abandoned adventure-seeking of the tactless Ram, they may not be able to appreciate the harmony of their differences any longer.

Aries - Scorpio: Here we have a meeting of two very different minds. And, in fact, a relationship between the Ram and the Scorpion often turns into a balancing act, though one supercharged with the fiery power of Mars, the ruling planet of both signs. They're a passionate, physical pair, with great potential for sexual commitment. Outside the bedroom, however, there could be trouble. Scorpio may not be willing to accept Aries's insistence on taking the lead. Aries's open desire to explore new territory may bring out the jealous, brooding side of Scorpio. If neither sign is willing to take a backseat, emotional turmoil in this relationship may douse the sizzling fire of attraction between them.

* * *

Aries-Sagittarius: In this two-sided ball of fire, both fire signs combine to form an action-oriented, enthusiastic couple with seemingly boundless energy. In Sagittarius, Aries has truly found its temperamental match. Both signs are impulsive, both combine wit and drive with a lively pursuit of a busy social life. These two live wires generally join in high voltage, pursuing a wide variety of interests. Sagittarius may take a more philosophical approach to life than Aries, however, and Aries tackles everything with a hands-on personal approach. Although hotheaded conflicts may threaten to short-circuit their electric bond, differences are bound to be short-lived.

Aries-Capricorn: In all likelihood, fire will energize earth in this match, with Aries emanating an enthusiastic aura that Capricorn cannot resist. Aries, in turn, is drawn to Capricorn's practical common sense, which is so different from the Aries impulsiveness. Both signs are cardinal in quality, sharing an inordinate sense of determination. And this allows them to ascend to new heights together, appreciating their differences instead of fighting over them. As one would expect, the Ram and the Goat are both assertive, and each is interested in achieving control in relationships, as in other aspects of life. For this to be a successful match, they must learn to cooperate rather than compete.

Aries-Aquarius: This astrological combination is a merry one to be in *and* to be around, with both signs active and fun-loving. Aries's unflagging energy will inspire Aquarius to dip into its idea fountain again and again to bring more original innovations to the relationship. They share a need for freedom and adventure. So much so, in fact, that they rarely quarrel for long. In one way they may be too much alike, however. Neither Aries nor Aquarius likes to be dominated. And with their fire and air natures combined, they sometimes become too lofty for their own good, and overlook little earthly details. If Aquarius can rely on its ultratolerant side, and if Aries can bring itself to exercise some tact, this relationship could blossom nicely.

Aries-Pisces: The first and last signs of the zodiac, this particular combination of fire and water is an odd one—for Aries and Pisces are each highly emotive signs, but in radically different ways. Aries finds the Piscean seductive, romantic imagination quite alluring, while Pisces is drawn to the Ram's dynamic, passionate energy. The fascination here is mutual, but the deeper these two partners go in a relationship, the more their differences are likely to be highlighted. Pisces is sensitive, intuitive and poetic, while Aries is direct, dashing, and aggressive. There is great possibility for balance but also for fundamental misunderstanding.

Taurus-Taurus: This is about the most stable, earthy, and sensual couple you'll ever meet. When two Bulls fall in love, the relationship is sure to be grounded, with each partner content to share in the other's love, reveling in their shared sensual pleasures and in the quiet, secure serenity of their home. Two Bulls together make for a doubly hardworking, loyal combination, so the Taurean streak of jealousy rarely has any occasion to flare. They do tend to be slightly shy—happy to quietly graze in their simple pasture of love. The greatest problems for this pair of homebodies will probably arise due to lack of stimulation, or clashes between their two extremely stubborn natures.

Taurus-Gemini: Although Taurus and Gemini differ in quality, polarity, and ruling element, a match between these two can be mutually beneficial. In this arrangement, sedate Taurus is catalyzed by Gemini's restless thinking, and volatile Gemini enjoys the rooted effect of Taurus's eminent practicality. Despite their intrigue with each other, however, the Bull and the Twins often miss each other at the deepest emotional level. The Taurus's need for a stable home environment simply does not mesh with Gemini's constant search for new experiences. In the long run, this pair may come across unresolvable troubles in their efforts to coordinate two very different characters.

Taurus-Cancer: A shared female polarity makes this quite a combination. Both Taurus and Cancer place strong emphasis on the pleasures of the home, and both are sentimental and passionate. The cardinal quality of Cancer gives the Crab an assertiveness that will in most cases direct this duo, adding a bit of spice to the otherwise staid Taurus. Moody Cancer can learn much from the many earthy, practical skills of Taurus, while Taurus benefits from Cancer's emotional tides, basking in the attention and caring the Crab loves to bestow. Over time, these two must guard against becoming annoyed with each other—Taurus with Cancer's powerful moods, Cancer with Taurus's predictability.

Taurus-Leo: Although quite different, these signs may enjoy a strong bond. Both Taurus and Leo, being fixed signs, are stable and self-contained, devoted to their careers. And their many opposite qualities will balance each other to a certain extent. The loyal Taurus sets a beautiful admiring stage for Leo's ambitions, for example. And Leo brings the couple outside of their own private existence and further out into the world than Taurus would otherwise venture. But Taurus must guard against being too stubborn, and Leo must learn to curb his all-pervasive sense of self-importance, or their intrigue will turn to a battle of opposites. Taurus will become critical of Leo's expansive, spendthrift ways, while Leo will think Taurus overly cautious and narrow minded.

Taurus-Virgo: This down-to-earth duo is a match made in heaven. In their own mild-mannered way, these two signs love each other and the world around them, admiring and fostering beauty. And they're practical-minded too. Not only do both signs tend to be skilled in arts or crafts, but both share a desire for financial security and have a strong streak of service in them. And Taurus's sensual stubbornness will prove a match for the rational, critical Virgo. Possible problems may lie in the too-similar nature of their personalities. Lacking a spontaneous approach to life, they may fail to stimulate each other and become too complacent, but neither one of them is likely to care.

Taurus-Libra: Under the overarching rule of Venus, Taurus and Libra would seem the perfect pair of lovebirds. Together they can openly share their love of art and music, but otherwise this relationship may prove to be a balancing act of opposites. Taurus will quite naturally answer to Libra's keen desire to find a balanced relationship. And Libra will thrive on the loyal faithfulness of

Taurus. But the flirtatious manner of Libra will only bring out Taurus's worst jealous streak, while Libra will criticize Taurus's inflexibility. They're both stubborn, and in matters of disagreement, will often engage in head-to-head combat.

Taurus - Scorpio: These two signs occupy opposite positions in the zodiac, but they are solid in their common fixed qualities, and complementary in many character traits. Scorpio is passionate, and Taurus supremely sensual, so when they get together in the bedroom, they merge into their own blissful world. They're both determined and ambitious, in relationships and in work. While this adds up to great compatibility, these two signs also have a tendency toward inflexibility, and must guard against cementing themselves into positions for too long. The combination of their two stubborn wills is bound to flare into anger from time to time, and when it does, Scorpio must take care not to sting, Taurus not to rampage.

Taurus - Sagittarius: While they have little in common, the Bull and the Archer may find their differences quite attractive. In their search for support and self-expression, each will usually draw the other to some middle ground. The serious, practical Taurus will help temper Sagittarius's wanderlust, bringing him a bit more down to earth. And the easygoing, uninhibited Sagittarius will help stir Taurus out of the Bull's more static state. Once that first wonderful stage of romantic euphoria passes, however, irritation often sets in with a vengeance. Possessive Taurus may be unable to cope with Sagittarius's wandering eye, while Sagittarius often feels aggravated by Taurus's unbending insistence on sticking to the same habits time and time again.

Taurus - Capricorn: In this sure-footed union, the solidity of the Bull is combined with the upward agility of the mountain Goat. Both are acutely interested in security, Capricorn even more aggressively so than Taurus. Once these two have achieved their little heaven on earth, in the security of hearth and home, Capricorn will turn especially warm, finally able to truly respond to Taurus's affectionate sensuality. They are a wonderfully compatible match, the only possible problem being that the straightforward Bull may find Capricorn a bit secretive. This pair must occasionally dig themselves out of their secluded romantic niche, shaking the earth from their settled ways in order to get at their deeper feelings.

Taurus - Aquarius: Though these two have very different outlooks on life, from time to time their dissimilar traits fascinate the Bull and the Water Bearer enough to bring them together. However, while their shared fixed quality may give this relationship some consistency, their basic disapproval of each other might very well outweigh their physical attraction. The unconventional Aquarius balks at the steady habits that are so important to the security-minded Taurus. And Taurus will be unable to bring this mate to appreciate the simple, hearty, sensual pleasures of the home. Taurus will raise a jealous roar at the constant Aquarian need to operate within a broader intellectual framework, working toward the betterment of society and friends. These two may have little staying power.

Taurus - Pisces: In this low-key pas de deux, the steady and sensuous movements of Taurus provide a successful complement to Pisces's poetic and private nature. Together, these two devoted, adoring signs meet comfortably at home, retreating from the world to a place where they both can muse on the beauty and tenderness of life. Generally, this is a mutually beneficial match. For Taurus honors the vulnerable feelings of Pisces, lending a steadiness to the shifting Piscean moods. Pisces, happy to sacrifice in the name of love for Taurus, gives the Bull the attention and control he thrives on. These two need to guard against tensions arising over Pisces's mystical bent and over Taurus's need for order, but these differences are usually surmountable.

Gemini - Gemini: When the Twins pair up, watch out! This pair travels in the fast lane, and is constantly racing to keep up with themselves and each other. Talk about quicksilver, these two seem to be in continuous change, enjoying a sense of mutual understanding as they explore the byways of their own minds and their relationship. They love to entertain and simply have fun, with the result that the Twin lovers will hold many a sensational party, keeping their jovial mood afterward as they move to their own private party in bed. As exciting as their adventure is, however, it also carries the possibility of danger. Deeper emotions too often go unexplored or unexpressed, and without a stabilizing force, their indecisiveness may occasionally swing out of control.

Gemini - Cancer: This is a duo whose profound differences—they share neither quality, polarity, nor ruling element—may initially bring balance to the relationship.

Cancer is so centered in emotion, and Gemini so focused in the mind, that each benefits from the other's style. But while both signs are prone to rapid change, the quality of movement is often quite different and more often than not leads to a clashing between the Twins and the Crab. Cancer's supersensitive mood shifts leave the Crab vulnerable to the flirtatious stance Gemini assumes toward others. The more cerebral Gemini needs change and variety to spark its intellect, and while Gemini is initially attracted to the very different Cancerean nature, the Twins are rarely capable of maintaining a steady interest for long.

Gemini-Leo: In this warm and especially lively combination, two very expansive, freedom-loving signs join forces. Leo cannot help but fire up Gemini's idea mill with its extroverted energy, while Gemini's perpetually intellectual side adds new dimensions to Leo's view of things. Leo may sometimes feel the need for a deeper sort of stimulation than the fun-loving Gemini Twins are used to supplying, however, while Gemini is not always willing to fawn over Leo with the adulation the Lion demands. Still, each is generally quite responsive to the other's sensibilities and nature. Few fights are in store for this pair, and those that do arise will be settled quickly.

Gemini-Virgo: This combination is a double-charged dynamo of mercurial energy, derived from their ruling planet, Mercury, as well as from their shared mutable quality. When Gemini's insatiable desire for variety is combined with Virgo's active mind, these two intellectual rovers get along famously. On other planes, however, Gemini and Virgo often have a tough time seeing eye to eye. Virgo's analytical, sensible attitude is often perceived as stodgy by Gemini; Gemini's need for different stimulation appears somewhat unorthodox and scatterbrained to Virgo. They each have very high standards to boot, and because of this, they can become overcritical of their differences. Long-term romantic success for this pair is unlikely.

Gemini-Libra: An exciting, well-matched couple, these two air signs will thrill each other with their natural penchant for mental exploration. Both these folks love freedom and fun, and won't tie each other down, for there isn't a jealous or combative bone in either one. Ruled by Venus, Libra brings its love-sensitivity to a couple otherwise dominated by thought. Together this couple tends to work in splendid, creative spurts followed by deep rest, taking time out for fun times with friends. Without this rest, nervous exhaustion may cause damage or lead to a tendency toward excessive indecisiveness. But generally, the match yields harmony and happiness.

Gemini-Scorpio: On a physical level, these two seem to be a great match. Scorpio's intuitive passion blends rather nicely with Gemini's imaginative exuberance, and their sensual compatibility often brings Gemini and Scorpio out beyond their normal boundaries. Emotional conflicts will probably override their sexual harmony once they leave the bedroom, however. Scorpio's jealous streak is aroused by Gemini's wandering attitude. Gemini cannot bear to forgo social evenings with lots of friends, which is incompatible with Scorpio's desire for privacy. Furthermore, lacking any earthly grounding, their relationship may be further weakened by their inability to deal with practical matters.

Gemini-Sagittarius: This pair of zodiacal opposites form one of the most deeply connected astrological combinations. Both Gemini and Sagittarius are mutable signs, changing their minds often, frequently taking mental voyages, and constantly exploring their many varied interests. A personable, outgoing attitude makes these two even more complementary, and they find each other funny and bright. But, under the elemental influence of air and fire, these two signs lack any contact with earth, and may have a difficult time dealing with day-to-day details, often choosing to ignore them. Practical and financial problems may become critical. And while their impulsive, freedom-loving ways draw the Gemini and Sagittarian lovers so magnetically together, this same attitude may eventually cause them both to seek new, fresher grounds.

Gemini-Capricorn: A quirky kind of balance can be achieved between the Twins and the Goat, one that works splendidly for both lovers. Since Gemini is at heart a promoter of new ideas, and Capricorn a practical climber, these two may very likely scale the heights together. They are ageless signs, so wherever they go, the Gemini-Capricorn pair will always be the youngest-looking couple in the place. But while both signs are united in their desire to influence others, Capricorn will take a conservative, routine approach to any project, while Gemini will act with an erratic, extravagant vigor that may drive the more conventional Capricorn to distraction. Also, neither one of these signs is given to undue sentimentality, and without special attention, their emotional life may never come alive.

Gemini-Aquarius: In this meeting of signs, Gemini and Aquarius can both feel free to shower their enthusiasm on ideas as well as on people. These two excite each other mentally, and they embark on an endless learning streak, constantly widening each other's horizons. Unlike Gemini, Aquarius does not indulge in the flighty, high-energy promotion of ideas, and this has a stabilizing effect on the relationship, helping to maintain the couple's strong intellectual balance. And while Aquarius is somewhat more preoccupied with reform on all levels—personal and social—the Gemini love of change can be adapted to this framework. Both these air signs are so socially oriented, however, that together they tend to fly over their emotional life, and thus need some sort of grounding.

Gemini-Pisces: With their shared mutable quality, the days and nights of this match are likely to be a complex, changeable sea of different moods. But while they may get along swimmingly in bed, their moods are often winding in completely opposite temperamental directions in other areas of the relationship, with Gemini constantly changing its mind, and Pisces its feelings. As Gemini wanders off in different directions, he may be unwilling to respond to the delicate Piscean sensitivity and need for affection, which makes the Twins feel hemmed in. And while Pisces may be stimulated by the Twins' insightful thinking, the Fish will probably also consider Gemini thoughtless and insensitive. Without some more dominant, steady influence, this combination may not last long.

Cancer-Cancer: In this doubly sensitive matchup of two Crabs, both lovers' interactions, with the world at large and with each other, stem from their powerful emotional side. Under the influence of their ruling planet, the Moon, these people are definitely subject to lunar phases and to each other's shifting emotional phases. A home-based couple, this pair is closely united by their deep, intense desire to nurture things, plants, and especially people. But with both partners so overwhelmingly preoccupied with their emotions, they are often unable to give each other the attention they need to reassure their sensitive souls. This could lead to a critical and demanding outlook that neither one is capable of changing.

Cancer-Leo: Both Cancer and Leo have deep, powerful emotions, and when they combine forces the mix seems about as unlikely as that of water and fire, their ruling elements. They are strangely compatible, though. In many ways, the nurturing, caring Crab finds the perfect romantic complement in Leo, who thrives on the attention and adoration of others. And the dominant strength of the Lion appeals to the more introverted sensitivity of Cancer, who's constantly on the lookout for an extroverted force to stabilize its moodiness. Both are serious and deep-feeling types, but they must be on constant alert to keep the opposite qualities of their feelings from extinguishing each other. These two are frequently fascinated by each other as friends, but get into troublesome misunderstanding in deeper relationships.

Cancer-Virgo: Although the analytical, intellectual side of Virgo differs greatly from the powerfully emotional personality of Cancer, this relationship may prove to be quite successful. The earthy, service-oriented streak dominant in Virgo is easily understood by the nurturing, maternal Cancer, although the Crab tends to take a more personal approach. Serving each other, they serve the world. These two also share a love of home and hearth, as well as a desire to strive toward financial security. On a more internal level, however, they differ greatly, with Virgo being exact, neat, and critical, Cancer being continually washed by splashing moods. Usually, this fascinates them, but in a committed relationship, this pair needs to guard against Virgo's nit-picking and Cancer's inconsistency.

Cancer-Libra: These two signs are joined by their cardinal quality, as well as by the humanizing influence of their ruling planets, the Moon for Cancer, Venus for Libra. But this union could turn out to be a rather unstable balancing act, with each partner contributing to the relationship on levels that are essentially different. Cancer acts in a never-ending swirl of the emotions that completely escapes the airy intellectuality of Libra. The indecisive, rather extravagant Scales are too detached and shallow for Cancer. Since a prime quest of Libra is a balanced relationship, and since Cancer is a creature of the home, these two might be expected to have a strong domestic life, but only if Libra can control the itch to pursue glitter outside the home. Although they might solve their differences in time, the chances for lasting happiness are slim.

Cancer-Scorpio: This is one truly romantic couple, with the Crab and the Scorpion both splashing the water of sentiment on each other. These intuitive, devoted signs both love to fall deeply in love, and will not stray from each other. Cancer's tender care will never give the Scorpion's jealousy occasion to rise, and is, in fact, just what the possessive Scorpio needs. And Scorpio's intimate strength will give the sensitive Crab the security he seeks. These two will revel in their co-created homey fantasy world. Affectionate and deeply thoughtful, there is great relationship as well as love here, as the passion of Scorpio and the emotion of Cancer join together.

Cancer-Sagittarius: When water and fire join together, the mixture must be carefully controlled and maintained if the elements are to successfully mix. Cancer, so cautious and sensitive and emotional, will have great difficulty understanding the more cerebral, outgoing nature of Sagittarius. The Archer, on the other hand, will feel frustrated and confined by homey, moody Cancer, and may unwittingly hurt the Crab with his constant search for outside stimulation. These two very different creatures can lend balance to each other, but only through patient understanding. Though there is often a mutual intrigue, in the end Cancer may not be able to put up with Sagittarius's wanderlust, while Sagittarius may find Cancer's moods too stuffy to endure.

Cancer-Capricorn: This cardinal couple of zodiac opposites is likely to be assertive, yet their relationship will be characterized by a strong emotional undertow. For although Capricorn is an earth sign, the reserved Goat has a sentimental side it tends to hide, and this secret world of feelings gives Capricorn and Cancer some alliance. While they are both good at handling financial matters, however, there are major differences between these two. Cancer feels slighted by Capricorn's ambitious preoccupation with work, and considers the Goat a bit too aloof. Capricorn is unwilling to give Cancer the constant emotional support the Crab demands. For this relationship to succeed, they must guard against Capricorn's calculating ambition and Cancer's periodic moodiness.

Cancer-Aquarius: These two combine a love of the old with a love of the new in a rather unconventional romantic liaison. Cancer reveres history and heirlooms, while Aquarius is drawn more toward the future and the latest trends. While passions may flare, as different as these two are it's not surprising that they have difficulty getting along otherwise. Aquarius, a believer in the profound power of logic, will often try to get the Crab to conform to his ideas. But Cancer's imaginative sensitivity will never operate on anything but an emotional level, and the Crab will resent Aquarius's efforts, and may feel insecure in the face of the Water Bearer's detached criticism. Because of Cancer's cautious side and the Aquarian quest for newness, this relationship may never really get off the ground.

Cancer-Pisces: This is a meeting of two watery souls. Both Cancer and Pisces are extremely emotional, with fragile, vulnerable hearts. But each is sensitive to the poetry of the other, each supremely caring in responding to the other. An intuitive couple, together, Cancer and Pisces are likely to make their moves from feeling rather than thought. Cancer, bringing its assertive, cardinal qualities to the relationship, will most likely be the decision-maker. Pisces, armed with the innate wisdom of all the signs that come before it in the zodiac, adds its dreams of the future, bringing an intuitive balance to this pair. If they can take special precaution against a tendency to wallow in their problems, long-lasting happiness is in store.

Leo-Leo: The energy radiating from this duo is so sunny and intense, you'll need sunglasses just to look at them! Two proud and stately cats rolled into one make for a glorious, majestic, passionate couple. This ambitious pair is a prize at any party, and they are just as interested in the adoration and entertainment of each other as they are in the attention of others. The only question is who will dominate, for nothing is harder for the Lion than giving room to another's ego, especially to someone whose sense of self-importance matches their own. These two will always express their emotions freely, however, and are honest about their arrogance. If the Lions can learn the art of compromise—no easy task—their passionate bond is second to none in the zodiac.

Leo-Virgo: Theirs is not exactly an even-tempered act. Virgo's cool, reserved personality is rarely in sync with the hot, passionate Leo. Occasionally, the combination of Leo's ambitious, gambling nature and Virgo's practical ability and clear vision will yield a productive, balanced relationship. But more often, proud Leo's tendency toward arrogant flamboyance arouses all the criticism of the more modest, intellectual Virgo. And Virgo's prudent ways hardly provide the sort of stimulation Leo seeks. Furthermore, Virgo is not as outgoing as the socially oriented Lion, and cannot bear Leo's egomaniacal, domineering ways. This affair is bound to be short-lived.

Leo-Libra: In this highly combustible couple, fire and air combine in a wonderful solution of enthusiasm and ideas. Together Leo and Libra will explore concepts new and fascinating to them both. Availing itself of the intuitive influence of Venus, Leo will keep this union in balance. Leo's passion appeals to the lighthearted, affectionate Libra, and their love nest will see plenty of hot, amorous action. Leo will be the dominant partner in this relationship, but Libra won't mind, since the Scales are good at sensing when to give. While this is a good match, their happiness may occasionally be marred by financial worries. Neither of these socially active types is likely to pay much attention to their spending habits until their bills catch up with them. Still, their romance may well flourish.

Leo-Scorpio: A supremely passionate pair, it's difficult to decide which is more saturated with desire, Scorpio or Leo. These two sensual dancers live with danger ever-present in their dance, however, with both signs aware that the mixture of their elements, fire and water, could snuff the action at any moment. A pair of fixed signs, Leo and Scorpio are equally stubborn in their differences. Scorpio's intense jealousy will most certainly be aroused by Leo's expansive personality. And the Lion will be infuriated by Scorpio's stubborn refusal to feed his enormous ego. Their past together is checkered, their future uncertain, but in the present they've got a love so good nothing else matters. Both are explosive and argumentative, and sooner or later the lid will probably rip right off this relationship, flinging both toward other romantic grounds.

Leo-Sagittarius: This is a supercompatible match in just about every way, a fiery joining of two personable, confident signs. Playful, passionate Leo strikes at the core of Sagittarius's need for exploration and adventure. They both love to go out into the world and meet new people, and each delights in open warmth from the other. This is one of the most fun couples on the astrological map, each possessing the confidence and enthusiasm the other needs. Sagittarius brings great wit and an intellectual strength that is not threatened by Leo's need to dominate. And Leo doesn't mind Sagittarius's wandering ways, and is willing to give the Archer room to breathe. This fiery pair may never burn out on each other, so absorbed are they by their shared adventure.

Leo-Capricorn: A relationship between these two may turn into a battle for dominance between their two equally stubborn wills. Leo is the king of the jungle, Capricorn king of the mountain. Their ambitions are manifest in such radically different ways that these two are bound to clash when they come together. Leo's unquenchable thirst for glory does not appeal to the more reserved, secretive Capricorn. Nor will Capricorn take a backseat to Leo, which will infuriate the Lion. Capricorn's persistence and security-minded attitude does not mesh with Leo's impulsive, capricious self-indulgence. The list of their differences goes on and on, and without the ability to give in to each other occasionally—which neither of these two is likely to do—this couple's future may be short-lived.

Leo-Aquarius: In this marriage of opposites, Leo brings warm, passionate qualities, while Aquarius tends to be more cool and impersonal. These differences sometimes form a deep link between these two signs, with Leo's fiery nature sparking the airy Aquarian imagination, and Aquarius's worldview helping to bring Leo out of its self-involvement. Over time, however, Aquarius's analytical, aloof side will fail to provide the unconditional adulation Leo needs. And Leo's dominant, egotistical attitude makes Aquarius feel stifled in its attempt to reach a broader understanding of his place in the world. These two may end up more irritated than in love with each other.

Leo-Pisces: When the Lion joins forces with the Fish, a meeting of very different elements, qualities, and polarities takes place—yet this union initially may have delicious results. These signs fascinate and somehow mystify each other, with Leo so social, Pisces so private; Leo so self-important, Pisces so self-sacrificing. When Leo's passion meets Pisces's poetry, this couple is in seventh heaven. But soon enough, Leo's active, public personality will clash with the introspective, mystical side of Pisces. The shy, vulnerable Pisces will seem a complete wimp to the more aggressive Lion, and Leo's fiery outbursts will be met by a submerged, withdrawn response. With two such different personalities, it will be difficult to make this match survive the test of time.

Virgo-Virgo: For the neatest, cleanest, most perfection-minded pair imaginable, just take a look at these two. The supercritical nature of Virgo means that both partners will hold themselves and each other to their extra-high standards. Together, Virgos in love form a very discriminating couple, practical in all things, and sharing great intellectual curiosity. Both are deeply influenced by the world around them, taking a very attentive, active interest in their environment. While neither is the type to explode in passionate flames, the serious side of Virgo also extends to a sensitive, responsible attitude toward the relationship. This pair may at times be a bit too quick to express criticism, but their closeness on so many levels will almost always override the critical tensions.

Virgo-Libra: When these two signs first meet, there is usually an enthusiastic bond between them. Since both Libra and Virgo are happy operating on a thought-oriented level, there is bound to be a meeting of the minds and much fascinating conversation. They share a deep intellectual curiosity. But beyond this, the similarities are few and far between. Serious, methodical Virgo loves to spend time at home, and won't be able to understand the more lighthearted, socially oriented nature of Libra. Nor will Virgo approve of the reckless spending habits of Libra. Libra, on the other hand, finds Virgo overly fussy and critical, too much of a stick-in-the-mud for his fun-loving tastes. With Virgo's often obsessive perfectionism and Libra's periodic indecision, these two will probably reach a romantic impasse before long.

Virgo-Scorpio: Virgo brings the mercurial tension of its ruling planet to this deep duo, and Scorpio adds the obsessive qualities of the far-flung influence of its ruling planet, Pluto. Together, the Virgin and the Scorpion form a very distinctive couple, whose differences somehow serve to offset and complement each other. The deep feelings of both signs, the shared concern with finances, and a solid home life will give their relationship stature and dignity. While the intense passion of Scorpio might be somewhat overwhelming to the more reserved Virgo, the imaginative side of the Scorpion mixes quite well with the intellectual, analytical nature of Virgo. Over time, Scorpio must find space for Virgo's addiction to order, Virgo for Scorpio's boiling inner nature. But these two are willing to work to maintain their romantic happiness, and quite often succeed marvelously!

Virgo - Sagittarius: A relationship between these two mutable signs is bound have a changeable quality to it. And, in fact, Virgo tends to move in accordance with its environment, while Sagittarius follows the many directions in which its fiery enthusiasm takes it. While this pair shares an intellectual bent, their very different outlooks on life may make it difficult for Virgo and Sagittarius to ever truly see eye to eye. Sagittarius is an eternal freedom-loving roamer, rarely devoted to only one mate for a long time, and he thinks Virgo's quiet, predictable lifestyle is much too restrictive. Virgo's strong, practical sense of order and responsibility dominates his view of the world around him, and so he is aggravated by the extravagant, impetuous wanderings of his Sagittarius mate. This match may not last long.

Virgo - Capricorn: Down-to-earth considerations and a mutual respect create a strong bond between Virgo and Capricorn. Both signs bring practical skills and a worldly, thoughtful outlook to the relationship. Both have a strong sense of home. Virgo will find little to criticize in the determined, ambitious Capricorn's style. Likewise, Capricorn admires Virgo's untiring industry and sense of perfectionism. Each provides the other with much-appreciated respect and approval, and there is every reason for this couple to stay together once they get together. But while they'll both openly share thoughts and ideas, these signs tend to be more reticent with their feelings. For long-lasting happiness, the Virgin and the Goat need to keep their feelings engaged and clear, learning to communicate on their deepest emotional level.

Virgo-Aquarius: A love of ideas and a fascination with intellectual pursuits is the linking bond between these two signs. Aquarius is the fountain of ideas, Virgo the steady waterwheel that puts those ideas to work. But the quality and expression of their minds is so different that Virgo and Aquarius may find it difficult to stay together for long. Virgo's view tends to be personal, his criticism directed toward individuals—including the self—while Aquarius is more expansive, keyed to helping all humanity. They are both cool, slightly detached, but in different ways—Virgo emotionally and Aquarius intellectually—lacking the outgoing passion necessary to draw each other to a more meaningful, shared understanding. These two will have to do a lot of work in order to establish a manageable partnership.

Virgo-Pisces: The Virgin and the Fish are often quite fascinated with each other—Virgo with the affectionate, emotional nature of Pisces, Pisces with Virgo's keen mental abilities. Both signs are rather chaste, and in their relationship they may sometimes engage in strong romantic love without great amorous activity. But despite the fact that these signs are rather retiring—not exactly party animals—the differences between the two may eventually drive them in different directions. As soon as hypercritical

Virgo finds any fault with Pisces, the supersensitive vulnerability of Pisces will render the Fish insecure and unstable. And Pisces, always searching for an ethereal, romantic lover, will be sorely disappointed by Virgo's unsentimental ways.

Libra - Libra: This affectionate act is doubly empowered by the alert and just qualities of the sign. Ruled by Venus, they are both loving people, sympathetic and charming, with a shared aim of harmonious love. But although this duo will easily achieve romantic harmony, reveling in their love of fun and excitement in the bedroom, there may be little balance in other areas of the relationship. Both signs have a lighthearted approach to things, and they tend to take a rather unrealistic approach to more practical matters. Without a more stable, balancing force, they could get carried away with superficialities, and risk a certain boredom in their lives. These two need to relax their desire to control situations that can never really come to a balance.

Libra - Scorpio: In this imaginative union, Libra is fascinated by the passionate intensity of Scorpio's expression, while Scorpio feels stimulated by Libra's airy, conceptual frame of thought. But when it comes to romance, Libra's enthusiasm is a bit superficial and fleeting for the more faithful, possessive Scorpion. And Scorpio's brooding moodiness and need for privacy irritate the fun-loving Scales. In all likelihood, when these two get keen on each other, they won't stay that way for long, for neither feels free to be himself.

* * *

Libra-Sagittarius: When the Scales and the Archer get together, the result is one brainy twosome. Libra brings intelligence and logic to the relationship, Sagittarius insight and wit. They both love books, teaching, and learning, and so are likely to turn their love nest into an innovative, exciting school where they both teach and learn from each other. There is great balance to this pair, as Libra feels stimulated rather than threatened by the impulsiveness of Sagittarius. And the Archer is willing to give more commitment to this relationship—which lets him breathe and wander freely—than to most. These two hold a nonstop ticket to romantic success.

Libra-Capricorn: In this cardinal combination, both Libra and Capricorn are aligned for control. But the means of their influence differ greatly, so when these two get together, look out! Capricorn will try to get Libra to adhere to his own materialistic, ambitious approach to life, causing the more impulsive, lazy Scales to rebel. And the Goat will simply not be convinced to attend the many social events that are so important to Libra. Capricorn's preoccupation with work leaves little room for romantic pursuits. Libra, on the other hand, will take a roll in the hay over a day in the office any day of the year. There may not be enough mutual understanding to see this couple through.

Libra-Aquarius: Libra and Aquarius get together in a meeting of minds, a confluence of idea streams merging into extraordinary vision. These two air signs stimulate each other into thoughts they've never had, exciting them in every dimension. Under the influence of Venus, the sentimental, artistic side of Libra tries to coax a more emotional response out of Aquarius—and sometimes succeeds. Both signs are extremely social, love to keep their calendars busy, and won't mind when their partner is constantly rushing out of the house, for they're both on the run twenty-four hours a day. Aquarius provides a stability to Libra's indecisiveness without cramping the Scales's style. And Libra, a natural diplomat, can handle Aquarius's stubbornness. If this pair goes out of its way to maintain a certain depth to its feelings, the relationship will probably last.

Libra-Pisces: This is a poetic pair, with Libra's sentimental, creative nature providing a fine complement to Pisces's ethereal, emotional personality. Libra brings clarity of thought, Pisces clarity of feeling, to the relationship. But in many other ways, there is little harmony. Libra feels constrained by the dependent vulnerability of Pisces, and may not always provide the romantic assurance the Fish needs to maintain his sense of security. Pisces doesn't understand the Libran need to venture outside the home for stimulation. Neither sign is very good about keeping tabs on finances, and together their monetary security will probably diminish. Temperamental obstacles are great in this relationship, and may override the sentimental, artistic pleasures they share.

Scorpio-Scorpio: When two of this sign get together, the result is one dynamo of a power pack. These two are intense, hypnotic, doubly passionate when they fall in love, joining their deeply sensuous desires. With Pluto as their co-ruler, both partners can easily become obsessive about their relationship. And while this can work wonderfully when they're in agreement, when they don't see eye to eye both will retreat to their brooding private selves. Outside influences can further break their bond, and any interest that both don't share will arouse Scorpio's intense jealousy. Because Scorpio is extremely adamant about all his opinions and feelings, this pair is bound to disagree sooner or later, and when they do it will be difficult for these stubborn, brooding souls to overcome their differences. For this couple to succeed, they must invest extra effort to strive for balance.

Scorpio-Sagittarius: In this energetic matchup, Scorpio's determined, passionate energy combines with the fiery, impulsive, insatiable curiosity of Sagittarius. Each of these powerfully emotional signs is easily attracted to the vitality of the other. Yet while their sensual, romantic explorations may flare, drastically different outlooks on life may make it difficult for the Scorpion and the Archer to stay together. Sagittarius takes the plunge recklessly, and is too restless and uninhibited for the more brooding, inner-directed Scorpio. Scorpio keeps his deepest feelings to himself and harbors a jealousy over the wandering mentality of his Sagittarius mate. Constant and candid self-evaluation is this couple's only chance for a happy life together—and even that may not keep them together for long.

Scorpio-Capricorn: This couple joins feeling and practicality to form one quintessentially resolute twosome. With Scorpio's determination and Capricorn's ambitious drive, when these two decide they'll do something, they do it, no matter what obstacles threaten to get in their way. The Scorpion and the Goat bring great balance to each other. They are both practical-minded and good with financial matters. Capricorn's need for security appeals to the dominant Scorpio, who'll rarely find any reason for jealousy. Like Capricorn, Scorpio has a private side, and this shared understanding allows Capricorn's hidden emotions to be roused by the more passionate energies of his Scorpio partner. In tense times, Scorpio needs to remember that Capricorn relies on daily order for support, and Capricorn needs to remember that Scorpio lives in a private world of emotion. But overall, this is a fabulous match.

Scorpio-Aquarius: These two fixed signs will initially find themselves in a potentially stable, satisfying match. Scorpio is drawn to the imagination and curiosity of Aquarius, while Aquarius loves the sensuality and intense emotions of Scorpio. But all too often, these qualities place the Scorpion and the Water Bearer in deep opposition rather than harmony. Aquarius enjoys its amiable quest for the mysteries of life—mysteries into which Scorpio has great, natural insight. Scorpio, on the other hand, is too private a person, too jealous and domineering to accept that the insatiable curiosity of Aquarius will often take the Water Bearer away from home. An air sign, Aquarius is emotionally distant and somewhat aloof, unable to understand the passionately expressed feelings of his Scorpio mate. Once the initial intrigue wears off, these two may not find enough in common to stay together.

Scorpio-Pisces: This is a powerfully romantic pair, for both partners embody an exquisite sensitivity. Scorpio brings the relationship innate wisdom as to the ways of life, while Pisces has a similar understanding derived from all the signs preceding it. Intuitive signs, both Scorpio and

Pisces are romantic and emotional. Scorpio is passionate and intense, Pisces gentle and tender, and they both love these qualities in each other. Scorpio's passionate, possessive attitude toward love appeals to the more vulnerable Pisces, who revels under this mate's protection. As the last sign in the zodiac, Pisces possesses an outlandish perspective that often piques Scorpio's enthusiastic imagination. The future looks bright for these two.

Sagittarius - Sagittarius: When two Archers hook up, their relationship is likely to resemble a sweeping romantic roller coaster. These two fiery, unstable lovers—each with an unquenchable wanderlust—are always on some kind of adventure, always certain that even better things lie ahead of them. Refusing to accept the seriousness of life, they dive headfirst into love with the same impetuosity with which they approach all things. They'll immerse themselves in an active social life, too, giving each other the freedom to explore new grounds. This impulsive, liberty-loving couple is not very adept at handling life's more practical considerations, however, and financial problems are usually on the horizon for them. Although ideally suited in so many ways, the adventure-seeking qualities that initially draw them together will probably also cause them to part sooner or later, each heading off in search of newer grounds.

Sagittarius - Capricorn: While these two are bound to have their differences, the Sagittarius-Capricorn couple is sure to be on the move. Sagittarius is on a never-ending physical, mental, or spiritual journey, while Capricorn moves steadily upward in his career, social, and financial climb. Together they blend two kinds of restlessness; Sagittarius brings its fiery enthusiasm, Capricorn its determination. Unfortunately, because of the different pace of their journeys, this combination may just as easily result in failure as in success. Capricorn—the logical, steady plodder—often resents the impulsive, shifting nature of Sagittarius's motion. Sagittarius, on the other hand, will have little patience for the security-minded, homebody ways of his Capricorn mate.

Sagittarius-Aquarius: The Archer and the Water Bearer make for a light and lively duo. Sagittarius, with characteristic enthusiasm and inquisitiveness, will invariably spark Aquarius's extraordinary breadth of vision, carrying them both to a romance of a new order. These two curious signs are bound to be keen on each other, thriving on each other's penetrating questions. And there's no jealousy in this relationship; since both love to keep up many outside interests, they'll give each other lots of room to move around. Sagittarius and Aquarius are both so busy exploring new ideas that their emotions may go ignored for long periods of time. In order to keep their relationship from floating on a superficial level of feeling, these two need to make a point of striving for a deeper emotional awareness.

Sagittarius-Pisces: Fire and water meet in this remarkable rendezvous. Like their elements, these two mutable signs are ever in a state of change. The imaginative outlook of Pisces suits Sagittarius's search for newness. But there are some fundamental differences between these lovers. Sagittarius is inclined toward philosophy and religion, while Pisces is an embodiment of poetic service. Sagittarius abhors the commitment Pisces needs, and has little patience for the vulnerable Piscean sensitivity. Pisces feels rebuffed by the roamings of the Archer, and searches for a dreamy sort of love it simply won't find in this partner. It will take a lot more than compromise to keep these signs in love for long.

Capricorn - Capricorn: With two determined climbers working together, this couple is sure to be a wonderful winner. Both partners are so practical, persevering, and ambitious that if they weren't so busy climbing, they'd be sitting on top of the world. While their united sense of ambition will leave them sitting pretty as far as finances are concerned, they may never find time together, for neither partner will be willing to compromise their work for any romantic considerations. Furthermore, without a more balancing, lighthearted influence, the Capricorn tendency to keep emotions hidden may lead to long bouts of brooding. These two are not an overly passionate pair, yet neither one is overly concerned by this. For long-lasting success, however, the Capricorn couple must learn to express emotion more frequently.

Capricorn - Aquarius: Earth mixes with air in this astrological pair. Steady and stable Capricorn can only gain from the stimulating ideas of Aquarius. And lofty, intellectual Aquarius will benefit from the practical skills of his Capricorn mate. If they can manage to keep a balance, this couple can bring to the world new concepts, backed by the determination they both share. However, Aquarius is always full of surprises, which doesn't always please the more predictable Capricorn. The Water Bearer is also a firm believer in self-expression, and will find himself continually aggravated by the self-contained brooding of

Capricorn. While these signs may get along famously as friends, they need to continuously remind themselves to compromise and learn to relate to each other openly if love is to flourish.

Capricorn-Pisces: In the case of this couple, when earth and water combine the result is sometimes stunning pottery, other times just plain old mud. Pisces is a meditative sign, with great imagination, and Capricorn an assertive, ambitious sign, so in cooperation, these two lend significant balance to each other. Capricorn provides the grounding Pisces needs, while Pisces has a romantic, idealistic outlook that helps balance the ever-practical Goat. And the Fish gives Capricorn an abundance of affectionate adoration, which keeps the Goat from sulking for long. When they're at cross purposes, Capricorn must remember that Pisces's most prized luxury is solitary musing, and Pisces must remember that Capricorn is programmed to climb. But overall, these two are quite well-suited.

Aquarius-Aquarius: For the most futuristic couple on the block, just look for a pair of Aquarians. Not only will they have such high-tech novelties as a solar-powered lawn mower and an electric motorcycle, they'll also dress avant garde, think avant garde, and behave avant garde. They'll both have many outside interests and plans. Aquarius is interested in people, ready to learn from anyone and everyone, so this pair will have many friends. And since neither one has an explosive or temperamental nature, these two will get along marvelously with each other. They tend to live on an exclusively intellectual, rational plane, however, and may ignore any emotions. While eminently compatible on all levels, Aquarians together must compensate for their top-heavy intellect by seeking additional psychic or emotional stimulation.

Aquarius-Pisces: This is an imaginative match, and the relationship between Aquarius and Pisces will frequently take a rather unconventional form. While both are imaginative people, Aquarius is quintessentially intellectual, while Pisces lives in a fluid, otherworldly sphere of emotions. Here, Aquarius gives forth an abundance of ideas, many of them eccentric, while Pisces receives and responds with a great intuitive sense of understanding. The ultratolerant, rational Aquarius is accepting of Pisces's private, retreating nature. And Pisces is tender and devoted, accepting the rigid psychological structure of the Water Bearer. Together they need to attend to day-to-day details, a difficult task for both signs, and promote their place in the world.

Pisces-Pisces: Pair up two natives of the last sign in the zodiac and you'll come up with the most otherworldly couple in the club. Religious and mystical, this emotional and sensitive couple is also exceptionally vulnerable. To protect themselves, they become adept actors when dealing with the outside world, adapting and concealing their true feelings. These two are at their best when they're off by themselves, where the Fish can give free reign to their powerful, intuitive imaginations and sentiment. Without someone to bring them down to earth, however, they sometimes get so far out they hardly feel any link at all with the practicalities of life. The supersensitivity of two Fish will find no balancing, lighthearted force in this partnership, and if one or the other sinks into a dark mood, look out!

CHAPTER IV

the Birth chart, your cosmic signature

Just as the DNA molecule contains your genetic code, so, too, does the birth chart contain your unique personal code. Your birth chart shows who you are and how you are likely to respond to life. It shows you your character in your Sun sign, your personality—the face you present to others—in your rising sign, and every other dimension of your being through the placement and relationships of the planets and other elements in the chart. Study of your natal chart reveals an ultra-high-resolution picture, fairly brimming with detail. Birth chart study will show you what types of men and women you most admire, who's best suited to you romantically, and what kind of person is most likely to be your ideal mate. Through such understanding, behavior and passions can be seen clearly in context, making it easier to take control of yourself and gear your actions to finding a romantic match that will last. The truth of the matter is, your soul mate could be of any Sun sign. And many factors in a birth chart could allow you to successfully team up with someone whose Sun sign seems to present problems to yours.

The birth chart is a map of the heavens at the instant of your birth, arranged astrologically. Perhaps the two greatest influences in your chart are your Moon sign and your rising sign, reflecting your emotional state and your personality—or the face you present to the world. These important influences are examined in greater detail in Chapter V. Next in importance are the planets. Each planet influences your personality or character, and the subsequent way you live your life. Furthermore, each planet's position has a specific influence on you, according to where it appears in your chart and how it relates to the other planets.

The chart is sectioned off into twelve pie slices, and each slice, or house, represents a different segment of your experience. If you have many planets in any given house, you'll have lots of activity in that area of life. For houses containing no planets, you'll have to make your own opportunities in the area of experience that house represents. All in all, the birth chart is a highly detailed map of you and your life. When searching for something as elusive as love, doesn't it make good sense to carry a map along?

Granted these maps are complex, and whether you have them cast by computer or by local astrologer, they may not mean much at first sight. You need to acquaint yourself with the map's symbols, then its structure. When cast, your chart contains planets, all scattered across your various spheres of experience. The planets exert influences, and their meaning becomes more specific when they appear in a particular house, under a particular sign.

Take Venus, for example, the planet of love. Venus gives clues about your feminine artistic self, and according to what sign it appears under, this planet can indicate varying attitudes toward pleasure and romantic relationships. A person whose chart shows Venus in Aries, the First House, will probably demand a lot of attention and affection in their love relationships, just as natives of that sign do. Someone whose chart shows this planet in Gemini, the Third House, may distance themselves from emotional romantic contact, just as Geminis tend to take an airy distance from most things. Likewise, Venus in the Fourth House, Cancer, means there will be a certain appreciation for the pleasures of a home environment. And Venus in the Tenth House, Capricorn, will add a lively, artistic influence.

Here, then, is an inventory of the planets, their symbols, and their ruling influences:

The Sun ☉ —the supreme power of the heavens, has the most power in your chart, indicating who you are, your character and purpose. It tells you what types of experience will hasten your personal growth, and what problems you are likely to encounter along the way. The Sun is one of the two luminaries—the Moon being the other—and it rules Leo.

The Moon ☽ —the other luminary, rules Cancer. Like that sign, this planet is centered in feeling and is much concerned with home life. The Moon also rules your persona, that mask by which you protect your most sensitive, emotional self. It represents maternal and feminine instincts as well.

Mercury ☿ —the ruler of Gemini and Virgo, stirs us physically and mentally, ruling travel and communication. It indicates the way you think and speak. Mercury rules the nervous system, as well as the mind.

Venus ♀ —the ruler of Taurus and Libra influences your soft, sensitive, loving side—the feminine artistic side. Venus is the mythical goddess of love. As such, this planet rules your love relationships and all that is beautiful, directing the way you respond to romance and the things you find most sensual. Not surprisingly, this planet strongly influences your ability to attract and relate to others.

Mars ♂ —rules Aries and Scorpio, with heat and dynamic action. This planet, representative of the masculine force of animation, provides a complement to Venus, which provides the fertility to make the Mars energy flourish. Mars influences the manner in which you handle yourself in the world. It is also the source of the sex drive—the fountain or lust that initiates the impulse to go out and seek a lover—and it indicates your general energy level.

Jupiter ♃ —ruler of Sagittarius and Pisces, is associated with growth—physically, intellectually, and spiritually. It is associated with boundless enthusiasm and, as such, is a giver of hope and good luck.

Saturn ♄ —called "the great teacher," reigns over Capricorn and Aquarius, and it is our sore spot. For learning is often accompanied by pain, and under the influence of this planet we are often faced with lessons we're afraid to learn. In its negative influence, Saturn retards natural processes. In its positive form, this planet is associated with hard work and organization, with your father, the teacher, and it indicates the process of lessons being learned.

Uranus ♅ —co-rules Aquarius, and was discovered at the end of the eighteenth century. At that time, both America and France were undergoing political revolution, and England industrial revolution. Like that period, this planet is revolutionary—in both upsetting and enhancing respects—and it is a planet of personal transformation. Uranus also indicates a uniqueness and an inventiveness.

Neptune ♆ —co-rules Pisces, and in mythology it rules the oceans. Like those fluid bodies of water, this planet can take on different characters, exert different influences. In its best form, Neptune indicates an inclination toward charity and good work. In its lower form, it tends toward deceit and cynicism. This planet also represents spirituality and mysticism.

Pluto ♇ —co-rules Scorpio, doing so from the farthest reaches of the known solar system. It is a planet of mystery, of social and individual transmutation. Pluto also exerts an obsessive influence.

These planets appear in your chart in various slices of the pie, and with that, have various influences. Below is a chart noting the different aspects of your life each house represents. Also shown is the sign of the zodiac associated with each house.

The twelve houses are phases of your potentiality, in increasingly sophisticated forms. The progression of houses marks your coming into self-awareness—seeing yourself, your family, your lover, your workmates, and the world. From the first to the last house, as you'll see from the chart below, the progression of the houses represents the natural flow of life, from your family, to playmates, schoolmates, and bedmates.

Three houses in particular warrant special attention in your study of your astrological love life—the Fifth House, the Seventh House, and the Eighth House.

In the Fifth House, you will find romance, fun, and all the good times imaginable. This house also rules your children, all sports, *and* your ability to play the game of love. It is the fun house. Here, you'll find pleasure that is strictly personal. And in doing so, you will bring into the world ideas and entities that will forever leave your mark. If you write a poem, your words will still be heard when you are no longer around to say them. The Fifth House is your personal game room, with pleasures from the most trivial to the most profound.

One of the greatest games in the Fifth House is romance, a game where prizes include not only happiness and pleasure, but growth as well. This is where you first learn of love, where you contact it as a child and as a young adult. It is also love in its most fleeting forms, such as flirtations, casual dates, and one-night stands. In this house, you're in your experimental stage, trying out partners and different ways of relating. It is here, too, where you discover your amorous abilities, the talents with which

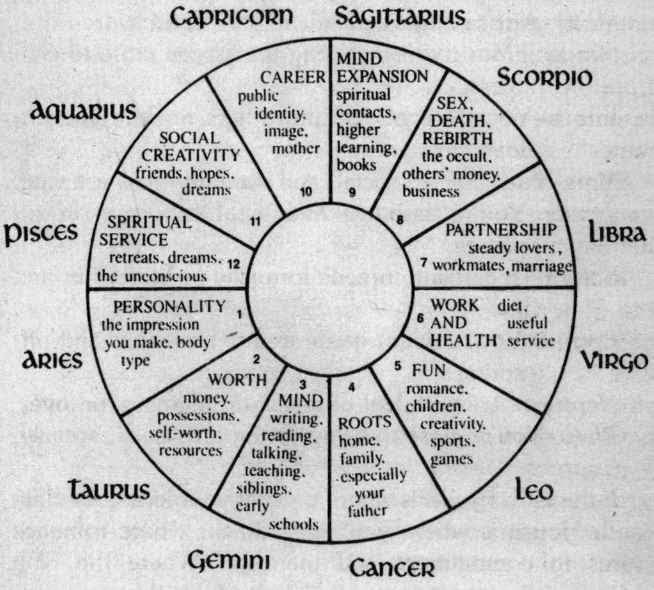
Capricorn
Sagittarius
Scorpio
Aquarius
Pisces
Libra
Aries
Virgo
Taurus
Leo
Gemini
Cancer
CAREER public identity, image, mother
10
MIND EXPANSION spiritual contacts, higher learning, books
9
SEX, DEATH, REBIRTH the occult, others' money, business
8
PARTNERSHIP steady lovers, workmates, marriage
7
WORK AND HEALTH diet, useful service
6
FUN romance, children, creativity, sports, games
5
ROOTS home, family, especially your father
4
MIND writing, reading, talking, teaching, siblings, early schools
3
WORTH money, possessions, self-worth, resources
2
PERSONALITY the impression you make, body type
1
SPIRITUAL SERVICE retreats, dreams, the unconscious
12
SOCIAL CREATIVITY friends, hopes, dreams
11

you give and receive love. You explore various depths, test your personal attractiveness. The ride often gets bouncy, but you're probably having a terrific time.

Take a look at the different characters each of the planets takes on in the Fifth House:

Sun-Childlike spontaneity leads to love and art.

Moon-Artistic affability leads to love and children.

Mercury-Music or storytelling brings you close to children.

Venus-Your love of self and others renders you endearing.

Mars-Your artistic, social, and romantic lives are vital.

Jupiter-You're assertive and theatrical, even in romance.

Saturn-Uncertainty breeds formality in friendship and love.

Uranus-You're avant garde in art, romance, and offspring.

Neptune-Artistic talent offsets your yearning for love.

Pluto-You're close to being driven artistically, socially.

If the Fifth House is where you get your kicks, the Seventh House is where you settle down, where romance turns to commitment and marriage. Where the Fifth House concentrated on your individual pleasures, the Seventh House shifts its focus to the pleasures of partnership. Here, dating has developed into a steady relationship, casual sex has become formalized marriage. In the Seventh House your love relationship has begun to serve a deeper purpose—for you and your lover, for the family you may have, and for society at large.

These are your very few close emotional relationships, those which require sacrifice and devotion if you are to continue reaping their treasures. In the Seventh House, you have gone beyond gratification into a lasting union which continuously breeds satisfaction.

The Seventh House is also associated with different ranges and depths of commitment. Here, then, is a place of great potential, a place of transformation where you might find not only personal fulfillment but social responsibility as well. The Seventh House is your mansion of marriage, and in it you live out the commitments you make to your mate, family, and society. May it be for you home sweet home.

Look over your Seventh House, noting the planets. Here's a short synopsis of those planetary influences in this mansion:

Sun-Tremendous emphasis on marriage leads to vitality.

Moon-Great need for emotional closeness leads to love.

Mercury-A mental union is more important than an emotional bond.

Venus-A charmer, you're great in groups, highly emotional in a couple.

Mars-You're sociable but erratic, loving but unreliable.

Jupiter-You're friendly, confident, and strategic, even in love.

Saturn-There is a great need for partnership, coupled with obstacles.

Uranus-Unusual forms emerge in love and marriage.

Neptune-You're often attracted to misleading love.

Pluto-You give greatly if your demands are met.

Finally, consider your Eighth House, the mansion of mystery and secrecy, where you develop an even deeper sensual, emotional, all-encompassing relationship with your partner. This mansion rules sex, conception, and birth, and it also rules magic, among other things. Planetary activity here can help foster an awareness of sex that is not only ecstatic, but also highly spiritual. In this form, sexual encounters are certainly still pleasurable, and are often even heightened. Moreover, from the emotional sensibilities this house engenders, purifying currents are stimulated, bringing the lovers a greater spiritual awareness.

Take a closer look at your Eighth House. Here's an indication of some of the planetary influences you might find in this mansion:

Sun-The power of your talents lets you stand tall and principled.

Moon-You have strong hidden emotional and sexual desires.

Mercury-The study of sex enthralls you.

Venus-Sex, wedded to emotion, leads to intensity.

Mars-You meet with all of life through sex.

Jupiter-You acquire either sexual, esoteric, or financial power.

Saturn-Sex is serious, but it presents obstacles.

Uranus-Sexual variety is considered important to you.

Neptune-You're imaginative in sex, mystery, and business.

Pluto-You're life is full of spiritual, sexual, or financial adventuring.

Suppose you don't have any planets in one of these houses, or—like an astrologer friend of mine—have no planets in *any* of them. Are you in for a flat, cardboard life, devoid of all romance? Is there nothing in this zone for you to work out, nothing to experience or enjoy? On the contrary! More likely, this might indicate that rather than experiencing an innate orientation to these situations, you'll come to them as they relate to other, more predominant influences in your life.

After considering the characteristics of the houses where the Sun, the Moon, and the planets are located, it is best to consider the larger patterns in your chart. Are there clusters of planets? Are they concentrated in a single house, or in one hemisphere? The top half of your chart may be thought of as your life of Doing, while the chart's bottom half represents your life of Being. If your chart is loaded with planets on the top, you can expect to lead a busy life in the world. If your chart is bottom-heavy, on the other hand, with most planets scattered through the first six houses, your orientation will be more inward, and many of the key events in your life may be between you and yourself.

Another overall pattern concerns the signs under which the planets are aligned, and from these, the balance of elements and qualities in your chart. If much of your planetary activity takes place under the influence of water signs, you can expect to be a sensitive, rather emotional type. Similarly, if there's a strong tendency toward mutable qualities, with more than half your planets showing this influence, you can expect to be a volatile person, ever in change. The more these details are considered, the clearer will be the picture of you that emerges in the birth chart.

You may also want to consider the aspects of your chart. Generally speaking, aspects are the phase of relationship between two planets, and they can exert a variety of influences upon a chart and hence upon a person.

Strong aspect patterns can dramatically alter your texture, offering tremendous opportunities for growth. However, aspects are somewhat complex and are best studied with the help of an astrologer.

Whatever you may gain from astrological self-exploration will help your chances for success in romance. Saturate yourself with the significances of your birth chart and/or the chart of someone you're drawn to. From the fostering of your understanding, love may be nurtured, life renewed.

The most specific and detailed information on the astrology of relationships can be gained through chart comparisons and composites. Chart comparisons, or synastry, call for the astrologer to list the location of all of your planets, as well as those of your partner. By comparing the aspects—angles between planets, which are either harmonious, in conjunction, or tense—of your chart to those of your lover's, this analysis will yield a wealth of information about your relationship.

Composite charts will also yield insight to a relationship. In these composites, your chart is combined with your lover's, divided in two, then reset according to your present place of residence together. Here again, the process is rather complicated, and it's best to consult an astrologer.

If you'd like to have your birth chart done, you can either contact an astrologer or order a computer-plotted chart. This last is available through several outlets, the most authoritative of which is

Astro Computing Services
Box 16430
San Diego, CA 92116
telephone: 619-297-9203.

CHAPTER V

YOUR MOON SIGN, YOUR RISING SIGN—FACES OF YOUR ROMANTIC SELF

There are many telling features in your birth chart, but two in particular have great bearing on your love life: your Moon sign and your rising sign. These both indicate faces of your romantic self, aspects of your being that lead you to and help you to relate to your mate.

The Moon in your chart indicates your basic emotional state, your attitudes concerning women, your mother, and mothering. It also shows, more clearly than any other astrological indicator, just what it is you cannot live without. Here is your consummate desire, a need so deeply buried in your psyche that your life will be unfulfilled and frustrated should you fail to satisfy it. And in many instances, the need is obviously love.

Through your rising sign, representing your personality, you meet and attract love. This is the self you put forward to contact the world, a version of you that has a specific look, a way of speaking, a manner of relating. This is your style, and it will be characterized by the sign that was ascending at the moment you were born. Your ascendant is also indicative of the kind of things you may yearn for. Scorpio rising indicates a desire for a good deal of sex, for example, while Libra rising may be characterized by a yearning for a balanced relationship.

Just as your rising sign shows the type of things you yearn for, your Moon sign shows the type of things you absolutely must have and how you must have them. For example, Aries, the youngest and most naive of the signs, wants your attention and wants it now! It's especially important to find out about your Moon sign, because it's one of the places for potential obsession in your chart, an emotionally vulnerable spot that could turn into your black hole, consuming all of you. When you live through your Moon, it seems as if that's all there is, this one all-encompassing desire. To keep it in its proper perspective, a little understanding can go a long way.

Your Moon sign also shows what kinds of women you admire, be they for role model or mate. Moon in Leo? You like the dramatic type, that sunny woman who's unafraid to be her glorious self. Moon in Taurus? You're more inclined to the perfect homemaker, an earthy person whose home is a sensuous haven. Whatever your Moon sign, these are the types of women that you want to be, and that your men want to be with.

If you have a computer chart or have had your chart drawn by an astrologer, check your Moon sign, then consult the following summaries. If you don't have a chart, you can find out your Moon sign from the table in Appendix A. Either way, you're about to reduce your lunacy while gaining an edge on your true emotional needs.

Moon in Aries: Emotionally powerful yet naive, these people need to control their environment. They are very loving, but only if they receive an abundant supply of affection in response to their own. Women whose Moon is in Aries tend to be domineering, while men with this Moon yearn for assertive partners. Both sexes have a tendency toward being self-centered, taking everything personally. Their passionate desires sometimes generate the heat of anger, as well as of romance.

Moon in Taurus: Championship-quality cuddlers, these down-home folks are a pure pleasure to snuggle up to, especially in the comfort of their own home environment. These are soothing, maternal, earthy people who need a secure home life. They love to touch, and make great listeners and fine mothers. Sexual fun here keeps the home fires burning.

Moon in Gemini: Information gluttons, these speedy souls tend to talk, think, and read their way beyond the emotions to a more intellectual plane. There's never a dull moment for these people, as they tend to change with mercurial frequency and suddenness. Needed first and foremost here is intellectual liveliness, even at the cost of emotional honesty.

Moon in Cancer: Home and family is where this heart lies, and all its emotional energies are attuned accordingly. Deeply caring, when these people give their love, it's forever. They will skillfully nurture you beyond your needs. Attachments form early and fast for these folks, with many of them maintaining close links with their mothers until late in their lives, consequently becoming maternal themselves.

Moon in Leo: These are child stars, performing gloriously in the ever-running drama of their lives. Those whose Moon is in Leo are show people, even at home, and plentiful theatrics make for a perpetually sunny program. Women with their Moon in Leo tend to be ambitious and radiant, while men with this Moon swoon upon meeting such females.

Moon in Virgo: Like the Virgin symbolizing this sign, these people embody a great sense of purity. They love order and cleanliness in both their physical and emotional life. They pick and choose their friends—and lovers—with great discrimination. Show them virtue, and they'll dote on you; but if you're crude, they'll turn away.

Moon in Libra: Those with their Moon in this sign need a balanced, stable relationship, and use substantial diplomatic skills to foster harmony at home. Occasionally such diplomacy runs roughshod over this Moon's real feeling, however, leaving these people in an emotional bind. Smart, soft, and kind, these lovers make fine bedmates.

Moon in Scorpio: Sexy and secretive, these lovers are so passionate they frequently hide their real feelings. They are generally reserved and seem quite mysterious until they grow more secure in your presence. Profound and creative, people with their Moon in Scorpio seem to live in a world of their own.

Moon in Sagittarius: Freedom-loving, these adventurous souls refuse to be tied down emotionally. Even physically, home is wherever they hang their hat, and wanderlust runs in a strong throbbing current through their veins. These lovers are fun and funny, but don't count on them for responsibilities or deep emotional probing, as they'd rather be off on the next adventure.

Moon in Capricorn: The Moon in this sign signifies a desire to acquire material security that is stronger than anyone else's in the zodiac. And these folks will go to extremes to ensure that security. Those whose Moon is in Capricorn are extreme emotional conservatives who find it hard, if not downright impossible, to show their real feelings. They often form relationships for material security rather than for passion alone. When the world finally measures up, these rather ruthless lovers reveal a wry wisdom.

Moon in Aquarius: People born with their Moon in this sign often need emotional independence, and to guarantee this, they may create unusual domestic arrangements. In this dawning of the Age of Aquarius, these people also need world unity, where men and women recognize each other as brothers and sisters in the realm of mankind. Bright and personable, they attract many friends and admirers, but resent any obligations.

Moon in Pisces: These people tend to be too sensitive for their own good. To offset this, they frequently retreat to the safety of home. But their sensitivity inevitably extends to love as well, and those with their Moon under Pisces really know how to pamper a lover, in and out of bed. Oases of kindness, they're compassionate and hospitable, needing always to be spiritually engaged.

As significant as your Moon sign is in your love life, your rising sun is even more influential. For as your Sun sign sets your character, the essential you, the rising sign sets your personality, the stylish face with which you meet and greet the world. Sometimes the Sun sign and rising sign are complementary in tone, sometimes not. A Leo friend of mine is Pisces rising, and so dominant is the ascendant, so different is the rising sign, that it took the longest time for me to met the Leo character.

The rising sign sets the tone of our public persona, the one we assume until we're absolutely certain we're in the company of a friend. It dictates how we're perceived by others, and what kind of first impression we make. It is directly associated with our body type and way of moving, our clothes and style of dress. Our rising sign, then, is the entirety of our display, that array of physical and psychological style that is the essence of our attractiveness.

All twelve signs rise every day for about two hours each, so your exact birth time is significant in determining this critical influence. If you have a chart, your rising sign can be found at the left-hand side of the horizon. If you have no chart, you can use the quick method described in Appendix B, or call a local astrologer or astrocomputing service.

Once you know your rising sign and your lover's, you can better understand what attracted you to each other, and what keeps you together. While the force, structure, and purpose of each of us comes from our Sun sign, the effects of the rising sign are what get us noticed. In romance, as in all other areas of life, it's important to understand the influence of your partner's rising sign for a more complete understanding of him or her.

The tone and style of the rising sign is similar to that of the Sun sign, but the form and influence of the two differ greatly. To refresh your memory, review the twelve signs described in Chapter II, then make the necessary mental adjustments to imagine those styles in personality, or the face presented to others, rather than in innate character.

The basic qualities of the rising signs are as follows:

Aries Rising: naive, brave, innocent, warm, and friendly.

Taurus Rising: gentle, questing comfort and security, stubborn.

Gemini Rising: given to talking and thinking, often with wit.

Cancer Rising: moody, maternal, and personable.

Leo Rising: self-assured, dignified, showy, and dramatic.

Virgo Rising: smart, shy, useful, meticulous, and worrisome.

Libra Rising: physical beauty, need for harmonious relationships.

Scorpio Rising: great willpower, sexual vibrancy.

Sagittarius Rising: optimistic, adventurous, charmed, and charming.

Capricorn Rising: ambitious, ever more youthful, tinged with sadness.

Aquarius Rising: cool, unique, socially and spiritually involved.

Pisces Rising: poetic, secretive, ultrasensitive.

Your Moon sign and your rising sign—two faces of your romantic self that guide you to love. A look into the astrological mirror will let you see these dimensions of yourself as they really are, enabling you to operate consciously in the realm of romantic possibilities open to you. Check your look, your style, your emotional needs, and frame them in the astrological context. Frame a friend, your lover, or a dream date. What you discover may just fill your sail with an exciting wind as you adventure across the ocean of love.

CHAPTER VI

Questing for Mr. or Ms. Right—Strategies for Tempting Fate

When looking to use your astrological understanding to great advantage in love, it's best to be able to use all of your intuitive instincts to sense the delicacies and nuances of a person's character. Add to this a logical framework, and a bit of savvy and motivation, and you'll soon be calling the signs like an old pro.

For a basic framework, consider the polarity of each sign. The six male signs—Aries, Gemini, Leo, Libra, Sagittarius, and Aquarius—are more active and extroverted. The six female signs—Taurus, Cancer, Virgo, Scorpio, Capricorn, Pisces—tend to be more sensitive, meditative, and home-oriented.

Whether you're playing the Sun-sign game just for fun or are quite serious in your love quest, a profile of each sign would help immensely in the search. It would be handy to know how your lover will look, dress, act, and speak as well as what they like to do and where they might be found. In reading the profiles that follow, remember that it would be simplistic to think that every person will fit the description, especially since the rising sign and other factors also strongly influence behavior, style, and dress.

To attract someone of a certain sign, you need to know what captivates them, be it in imagination, intellect, feeling, or physicality. Realizing what truly turns them on, you can go about being the embodiment of that turn-on.

Aries: Look for a bold, bright dresser, especially partial to reds. The fiery, egotistical nature of this sign begs for attention, so to win favor, pay great attention. This dashing, enterprising character is frequently found in leadership positions. Idealistic and original, you'd sooner find this one competing in a triathlon than bowling. A pronounced brow and a narrow bridge lend Ram-like appearance to the face. This is an active, entrepreneurial type, one you meet heading his or her own business, or out in the world soaking up the latest culture. To attract such a person, ask their advice about almost anything.

Aries's erogenous zone is the head and face, and you can set a Ram on fire by lavishing attention on these areas, gently stroking their sensitive lips and cheeks, kissing their eyelids, and playing with their hair. A relaxing scalp massage is another surefire way to put an Aries in an amorous mood.

Taurus: If you look around for the strong, silent type, often dressed in earth tones, chances are you'll come across a Taurean. These great sensualists love jewelry, perfume, and finery, though their dress can be very practical as well. Greens and browns dominate their color schemes, in clothing and decor. Home is where the heart is, and this type is easiest to meet at a small party or a friend's house. They like to eat, are impressed by bigness, and have a bovine quality, especially about the eyes. They're funny, too, operating in a low tempo. And because they're ruled by Venus, they love to love and are great admirers and creators of beauty. You'll meet them near the earth—gardening, sculpting, or potting—or you might hear them singing as they work, bathe, or perform. To attract such a person, sing a song, show an interest in wildlife, or rent a big summer house.

Taurus rules the throat and neck, and the Bull is extremely aroused by erotic stimulation of this area. Planting tantalizing kisses along the column of your Taurus lover's throat, stroking his long, expressive neck, and nibbling on his nape will place Taurus at your mercy.

Gemini: It's easy to recognize a Gemini. Just look for speedy exuberance in a very youthful act, for these high-velocity talkers and thinkers never seem to age. They tend to dress in yellows, greens, and blues, and because of their mutable, mercurial nature, they change outfits frequently. With their restless minds, look for this sign at the library or out promoting their latest idea. Many people born under this sign become writers, orators, journalists, lawyers, or computer wizards. To balance their highly nervous energy, these people somehow know they must walk or run in the fresh air, so you'll also find Geminis outdoors. Since talking and reading are two of this one's favorite activities, a conversation about the latest book you're reading might be fun for both of you. But remember, Geminis make bad listeners and would much rather do the talking, so be the perfect foil, asking the right questions, letting them dominate the conversation.

A Gemini's shoulders, arms, and hands are the most sensitive to a lover's touch. Kiss his wrists, his palms, the insides of his forearms, traveling slowly up the length of his arm to his shoulders. Brushing the hands and arms with your fingertips is another way to make a Gemini burn with desire.

Cancer: Physically, Cancer is characterized by either a roundish, Moon face or a heavy-browed, crab-shaped face, both pleasing and sympathetic. These caring people go through many moods and, despite their assertive ways in the world, they are very attached to their homes. Cancereans tend to dress in Moon tones—pale gold and green, and also pale lavender. They love to hear a good joke and will always have a few to tell in return. These people love the water and often live near it, making it the center of their activity. You'll find them swimming, fishing, boating, water skiing, and scuba diving. To attract such a person, tell a good joke they can overhear, offer them food, or strike up a conversation about history.

Cancer rules the breasts and stomach, and the breasts are Cancer's erogenous zone. Male and female Cancereans alike are particularly aroused by a lover's oral and manual stimulation of this incredibly sensitive area, especially the nipples. Kissing and caressing a Cancer female's breasts or a Cancer male's chest will set the Crab on fire!

* * *

Leo: People of this Sun sign have a proud, dignified bearing. Typically, they are given to dressing in gold, red, and other regal colors suitable to their brilliance. These people love to be at center stage, and you can find them performing in the theater, or in the middle of their crowd of friends. Passionate, they tend to overspend their emotions dramatically. Flatter these cats, and they'll purr. To attract a Leo, be dramatic and majestic yourself, or be an adoring fan.

Proud Leo rules the spine, back, and heart, and massaging a Leo's back will definitely put him in the mood for love! Sweeping caresses, running your finger along the length of his spine, and paying particular attention to the sensitive small of the back will relax your Leo lover and sexually excite him.

Virgo: You'll have no trouble recognizing this sign. If you spot a fastidious dresser, clothed especially in browns, greens, and blues, you'll have found a Virgo. Despite a quiet intensity, these people have soothing eyes and a calming manner about them. They are frequently wiry in build and usually untiring in their efforts. They adore cats, which are ruled by Virgo, and this makes an excellent subject for conversation with them. But be warned: Virgoans hate gushy sentimentality. They are industrious and productive before all else, often working as editors, critics, or in the arts. They're rarely idle, so don't go looking for this sign at the local hangouts and bars. Instead, make the most of your business encounters with this sign. Or you might have to go look in the woods for this one, as this is the sign of the holy hermit. They practically worship utility, so in order to attract such a person, show them how useful you can be, or let them see you feed some stray cats.

Virgo rules the nervous system and intestines. Paying particular erotic attention to the stomach area, stroking, kissing, and caressing the abdomen is sure to arouse your Virgo lover's passion. Since they're so attracted to cleanliness, Virgos will also find a playful bath tantalizing.

Libra: This sign will always seem a charming and extremely diplomatic type, often dressing in a balance of color, from mauve to blue. Librans are honorable, sympathetic people who bring even enemies together. They love books, and fascinating literary conversations enthrall them. So pick a book, any book, and bring it up in your conversations with a Libran. Your discussion is bound to be a hit with both of you. Ruled by Venus, these people are programmed for love. They are very loving, but they need to be loved, too, so don't hesitate to show any affection or appreciate you feel for them. You'll find them in libraries, in the publishing field, and in law—wherever they have a chance to use their keen minds to balance things out. In order to attract such a person, wave a best-seller their way, show a little tenderness, and allow yourself to be charmed.

Libra's erogenous zone is the lower back and buttocks, and Librans love to have their buttocks fondled, pinched, and patted. Lavish gentle, teasing caresses on a Libran's lower back, and massage the entire back and buttocks area. Libra will soon be under your sexual spell.

Scorpio: To find a Scorpio, look for a dignified, determined person whose insides boil while the face remains frozen. There is an aura of intense virility surrounding this sign, in both men and women. A rich burgundy color corresponding to Pluto is the preferred color of most Scorpions, but they also dress in various other reds, in accord with the influence of their principal ruler, Mars. Because of their fascination with the mysterious, you'll find these people being psychologists, astrologers, and detectives. They're sexy, and there's an electricity to them. So to attract such a person, transform yourself into an enigma shrouded in mystery, or show your passion . . . in any way, about any thing.

Scorpio rules the genitals, and while the genitals are an erogenous zone for everyone, Scorpio's intense sexual focus is centered in this area. Slowly, teasingly stroking a Scorpio's genitals and the tender areas around them is the key to unleashing his tremendous passion.

Sagittarius: If you come across an impulsive, restless soul—one who must have freedom at all costs—chances are you've found a Sagittarian. Sometimes this sign will sport purple pants or a purple necktie. These people are inclined toward science, religion, and philosophy, and they make excellent teachers. But their inability to endure stale or stuffy spots sends them outdoors a lot, and they're great sports. You'll find Sagittarians on the playing fields, engaged in baseball, football, tennis, and golf. They love nature too, and you can often catch them on the trail, or canoeing down a local river. To attract such a person, become a friendly travel expert, as these people have a heavy case of wanderlust. Or be adventurous toward them, as they love adventure.

The hips and thighs are the erogenous zones of Sagittarius. Give your Sagittarian lover an erotic massage on his upper legs, or tease him with light nibbles, kisses, and caresses along the insides of his thighs. The Centaur will shiver with delight!

Capricorn: Capricorn is a serious and reserved social climber, who often dresses in the dark hues of black and blue, or brown and green. These ambitious types tend to excel, especially in business. Fast climbers, they court success. To be of interest to them you must offer them a way up the ladder, be it socially or financially. Only after they've reached some security with you will they open up about any emotion. You'll find them in places of high culture—in museums and at concerts, for instance. To attract such a person, let them overhear stories of your success, or ask their opinion in a matter of tradition.

Capricorn rules the bones, knees, teeth, and joints, and this sign's special erogenous zone is the knees. Fondling and caressing the knees, using your lips, your hands, and the tips of your fingers, will drive your Capricorn love wild!

Aquarius: This sign is an amiable, ultratolerant type who enjoys shocking folks who are more conventional than he. There's a nobility to the profile of an Aquarian, both physically and psychologically. They absolutely demand personal freedom and are often just ahead of the latest trends. Similarly, their dress is likely to be avant garde—or at the very least quite stylish—and they favor sapphire and other blues. Ideas are their magic medium, and you can find these people in politics, in the theater, in their writing studios, or in their invention laboratories. To attract such a person, invent anything, from a word to a gesture to a gizmo, or do something surprising.

Aquarians are particularly sensitive around the calves

and ankles. Touching and kissing this area will send shivers up a Water Bearer's spine. Try massaging the calves with fragrant oils, or a warm, soapy sponge. And contact with the calves or ankles while making love heightens Aquarius's pleasure.

Pisces: Pisces is always a laid-back, poetic type who observes the world with extreme tenderness. Those born under this sign are sensitive people, always flowing, always slightly subdued, as if they'd seen too much. They're often artists, and because of their acute sensitivity, need to retreat from the world to a safe refuge. Dressing in tones of emerald and aquamarine, these people touch others with the depths of their devotion, and are also found in politics, religion, and on stage. To attract such a person, do charity work, or start a conversation on some mystical topic with them.

Pisces rules the feet and toes, and Pisceans are erotically aroused by relaxing foot massages and by having their feet gently soaked in warm, scented water. Pay special attention to the arch and the toes. Relaxing your Pisces lover's feet will relax his whole body and dramatically increase his sexual desire.

CHAPTER VII

From Celestial Harmony to Domestic Tranquility

If you're lucky enough to be involved in domestic life with a lover, be thankful. Many people yearn for such committed closeness, so if you have a working love, treasure and protect it. Armed with an astrological understanding of yourself and your mate, you'll probably be able to find the patience, tolerance, and generosity often needed to make a relationship work. Keep in mind that the marriage of any two signs will have beneficial possibilities. You and your lover will always be in a state of evolution, and it's important to know how your bonds may shift to keep things on an even keel.

Frustration and confusion may visit anyway, but with astrological insight, romantic obstacles might be kept to a minimum. If you're a Virgo, for example, and realize that your supercritical faculties always focus on the flaws in others, this realization may allow you to back off your mental monologue and consider that this apparent intelligence is really *your* flaw, not your lover's.

Insight can be added from Sun-sign compatibility study, turning the focus to the probable strengths and weaknesses of your match to find out what can be done to emphasize the former, compensate for the latter. Noting the potentialities and pitfalls, you and your lover can consciously opt for the evolved long-term course of commitment, one which inevitably leads to fulfillment. For example, if you and your lover were born under the same sign, your attraction is obvious—the two of you will act like a mini-society of mutual admiration. You have the same style, the same value system and outlook. There is immediate and deep understanding, empathy at its most profound. At the same time, because you're so similar, the relationship will probably have some imbalances. Your weaknesses will be compounded, your strengths overemphasized. If you two are not careful, you can become ingrown, convinced of the dominance of your style, stifling each other for lack of stimulation.

But if fascination turns to frustration in your love nest, use celestial navigation, sight on the stars to rechart your course. If you know where you are and where you're headed, much needless anxiety can be eliminated. Intelligent course alterations can be made to avert possible danger and unhappiness. As co-captain of your joint vessel, you can help keep your relationship in calm waters, heading for maximum smooth sailing. In turbulent conditions, couples frequently veer off course. But if you're attentive to all signs of change, constantly noting the attitude of your joint vessel, even in foul weather you'll be able to keep your love clear of the rocks.

In order to maintain a heavenly and orderly relationship you've got to tend your Seventh House, the mansion of partnership and marriage. Examine your Seventh House, and the Seventh House of your lover. Are there correspondences between your planetary activity there and your lover's? Note the signs of the planets in this house. Does your lover embody any of the characteristics implied by those signs? Also, if your partner's Sun sign or rising sign matches any of those signs, that planet's influence will be all the stronger. Even if the correspondences you find don't reflect perfect harmony with the influences obvious in your own chart, you can still have a fulfilling relationship . . . with a little extra effort.

Such revelations can be instructive as well as tension-relieving. They can help explain your expectations, your reservations, and secret criticisms. Just as the stars give insight into your character and personality, they also set in you a preference for a certain type of mate. Should your lover be just your preferred type, so much the better. Here again, though, if the stars do not line up perfectly, astrology shows the way to use its insights to foster celestial harmony in earthly love.

CHAPTER VIII

heaven help you, and your lover

In a relationship, you continuously rediscover yourself. Through astrology, you and your partner can both see what your tendencies are when you're together. You'll find happiness in your relationship's strengths, and the know-how to help you both change things for the better. As an operating couple, the opportunities to help maintain mutual happiness and emotional and sexual fulfillment are many, the possibilities for individual and collective growth tremendous. Together, you can balance each other and harmonize. Together, you can investigate your destiny, guided by the stars and by your own intelligence.

The twelve houses on your birth chart represent the varieties of earthly experience. Simply recognizing the various types of experience can allow you to see your life as never before. Patterns will become clear, behavior will become comprehensible.

In all likelihood, your lover will provide some balance for you. As if they were weights on a wheel, your mate's planets will exert influences on you, adding to your circle of experience. With your own chart as a guide, you can make great use of these influences. By learning where you are naive, you'll be able to strengthen your knowledge in those areas if your mate is strong in them. It is through your lover's catalytic effect that you can develop the fullness of yourself. In doing so, you not only enrich yourself, but your lover and the world as well.

It takes only a single meeting to turn your love life around. And you must constantly keep yourself open to encounters likely to lead to romantic success. Astrology provides the knowledge to draw upon to help your romantic fate along. Playfully explore your motivations and those of your love in an astrological context. It's sure to be a revealing and fun exercise. With astrology as your guide, you and your lover can discover sides of yourselves you never before knew existed, evolving as you dance the night away together.

There is no absolutely star-crossed love, not even Romeo and Juliet's. They had their chances, and you, too, will have many. So take a long look at your stars. With the heavens to help, you and your lover can star in your real-life romance.

APPENDIX A

moon tables

To determine your Moon sign, find the table of your year of birth. Then find the column for your birthday month; and finally—because the tables list the dates the Moon *moved into* a new sign—find the date closest, *but not after*, your birthday. For example, if you were born September 12, 1963, find the year 1963 and the "SEP" column. It shows that on September 11, 1963, the Moon moved into Cancer, and on September 13 it moved into Leo, so your sign is Cancer. Note: If a Moon moved into a new sign on your birthday, you may have been born in the previous day's sign. Read the descriptions for both signs to determine which is yours.

1940

JAN	FEB	MAR	APR	MAY	JUN
1 LIB	1 SAG	2 CAP	1 AQU	3 ARI	2 TAU
3 SCO	4 CAP	4 AQU	3 PIS	5 TAU	4 GEM
5 SAG	6 AQU	7 PIS	6 ARI	8 GEM	6 CAN
7 CAP	9 PIS	9 ARI	8 TAU	10 CAN	9 LEO
10 AQU	11 ARI	12 TAU	11 GEM	12 LEO	11 VIR
12 PIS	14 TAU	14 GEM	13 CAN	15 VIR	13 LIB
15 ARI	16 GEM	17 CAN	15 LEO	17 LIB	15 SCO
17 TAU	18 CAN	19 LEO	17 VIR	19 SCO	17 SAG
20 GEM	20 LEO	21 VIR	19 LIB	21 SAG	19 CAP
22 CAN	22 VIR	23 LIB	21 SCO	23 CAP	22 AQU
24 LEO	24 LIB	25 SCO	23 SAG	25 AQU	24 PIS
26 VIR	26 SCO	27 SAG	26 CAP	28 PIS	27 ARI
28 LIB	29 SAG	29 CAP	28 AQU	30 ARI	29 TAU
30 SCO			30 PIS		

1941

JAN	FEB	MAR	APR	MAY	JUN
1 PIS	2 TAU	2 TAU	1 GEM	3 LEO	1 VIR
4 ARI	5 GEM	4 GEM	3 CAN	5 VIR	4 LIB
6 TAU	7 CAN	7 CAN	5 LEO	7 LIB	6 SCO
9 GEM	10 LEO	9 LEO	8 VIR	9 SCO	8 SAG
11 CAN	12 VIR	11 VIR	10 LIB	11 SAG	10 CAP
13 LEO	14 LIB	13 LIB	12 SCO	13 CAP	12 AQU
15 VIR	16 SCO	15 SCO	14 SAG	15 AQU	14 PIS
18 LIB	18 SAG	17 SAG	16 CAP	18 PIS	16 ARI
20 SCO	20 CAP	19 CAP	18 AQU	20 ARI	19 TAU
22 SAG	23 AQU	22 AQU	20 PIS	23 TAU	21 GEM
24 CAP	25 PIS	24 PIS	23 ARI	25 GEM	24 CAN
26 AQU	27 ARI	27 ARI	25 TAU	28 CAN	26 LEO
29 PIS		29 TAU	28 GEM	30 LEO	29 VIR
31 ARI			30 CAN		

1940

JUL	AUG	SEP	OCT	NOV	DEC
2 GEM	2 LEO	1 VIR	2 SCO	1 SAG	2 AQU
4 CAN	4 VIR	3 LIB	4 SAG	3 CAP	5 PIS
6 LEO	6 LIB	5 SCO	6 CAP	5 AQU	7 ARI
8 VIR	9 SCO	7 SAG	9 AQU	7 PIS	10 TAU
10 LIB	11 SAG	9 CAP	11 PIS	10 ARI	12 GEM
12 SCO	13 CAP	11 AQU	14 ARI	13 TAU	15 CAN
14 SAG	15 AQU	14 PIS	16 TAU	15 GEM	17 LEO
17 CAP	18 PIS	16 ARI	19 GEM	17 CAN	19 VIR
19 AQU	20 ARI	19 TAU	21 CAN	20 LEO	21 LIB
21 PIS	23 TAU	22 GEM	23 LEO	22 VIR	23 SCO
24 ARI	25 GEM	24 CAN	26 VIR	24 LIB	26 SAG
26 TAU	28 CAN	26 LEO	28 LIB	26 SCO	28 CAP
29 GEM	30 LEO	28 VIR	30 SCO	28 SAG	30 AQU
31 CAN		30 LIB		30 CAP	

1941

JUL	AUG	SEP	OCT	NOV	DEC
1 LIB	1 SAG	2 AQU	1 PIS	2 TAU	2 GEM
3 SCO	3 CAP	4 PIS	4 ARI	5 GEM	5 CAN
5 SAG	5 AQU	6 ARI	6 TAU	7 CAN	7 LEO
7 CAP	8 PIS	9 TAU	9 GEM	10 LEO	10 VIR
9 AQU	10 ARI	11 GEM	11 CAN	12 VIR	12 LIB
11 PIS	13 TAU	14 CAN	14 LEO	15 LIB	14 SCO
14 ARI	15 GEM	16 LEO	16 VIR	17 SCO	16 SAG
16 TAU	18 CAN	19 VIR	18 LIB	19 SAG	18 CAP
19 GEM	20 LEO	21 LIB	20 SCO	21 CAP	20 AQU
21 CAN	22 VIR	23 SCO	22 SAG	23 AQU	22 PIS
24 LEO	24 LIB	25 SAG	24 CAP	25 PIS	24 ARI
26 VIR	26 SCO	27 CAP	26 AQU	27 ARI	27 TAU
28 LIB	28 SAG	29 AQU	29 PIS	30 TAU	29 GEM
30 SCO	31 CAP		31 ARI		

1942

JAN	FEB	MAR	APR	MAY	JUN
1 CAN	2 VIR	1 VIR	2 SCO	2 SAG	2 AQU
3 LEO	4 LIB	4 LIB	4 SAG	4 CAP	4 PIS
6 VIR	7 SCO	6 SCO	6 CAP	6 AQU	6 ARI
8 LIB	9 SAG	8 SAG	8 AQU	8 PIS	9 TAU
10 SCO	11 CAP	10 CAP	11 PIS	10 ARI	11 GEM
12 SAG	13 AQU	12 AQU	13 ARI	13 TAU	14 CAN
14 CAP	15 PIS	14 PIS	15 TAU	15 GEM	16 LEO
16 AQU	17 ARI	17 ARI	18 GEM	18 CAN	19 VIR
19 PIS	20 TAU	19 TAU	20 CAN	20 LEO	21 LIB
21 ARI	22 GEM	21 GEM	23 LEO	23 VIR	23 SCO
23 TAU	25 CAN	24 CAN	25 VIR	25 LIB	25 SAG
26 GEM	27 LEO	26 LEO	27 LIB	27 SCO	27 CAP
28 CAN		29 VIR	30 SCO	29 SAG	29 AQU
31 LEO		31 LIB		31 CAP	

1943

JAN	FEB	MAR	APR	MAY	JUN
1 SCO	1 CAP	1 CAP	1 PIS	3 TAU	1 GEM
3 SAG	3 AQU	3 AQU	3 ARI	5 GEM	4 CAN
5 CAP	5 PIS	5 PIS	5 TAU	7 CAN	6 LEO
7 AQU	7 ARI	7 ARI	8 GEM	10 LEO	9 VIR
9 PIS	10 TAU	9 TAU	10 CAN	12 VIR	11 LIB
11 ARI	12 GEM	11 GEM	13 LEO	15 LIB	14 SCO
13 TAU	14 CAN	14 CAN	15 VIR	17 SCO	16 SAG
16 GEM	17 LEO	16 LEO	18 LIB	19 SAG	18 CAP
18 CAN	19 VIR	19 VIR	20 SCO	21 CAP	20 AQU
21 LEO	22 LIB	21 LIB	22 SAG	23 AQU	22 PIS
23 VIR	24 SCO	23 SCO	24 CAP	26 PIS	24 ARI
26 LIB	26 SAG	26 SAG	26 AQU	28 ARI	26 TAU
28 SCO		28 CAP	28 PIS	30 TAU	29 GEM
30 SAG		30 AQU	30 ARI		

1942

JUL	AUG	SEP	OCT	NOV	DEC
1 PIS	2 TAU	1 GEM	1 CAN	2 VIR	2 LIB
4 ARI	5 GEM	4 CAN	4 LEO	5 LIB	4 SCO
6 TAU	7 CAN	6 LEO	6 VIR	7 SCO	6 SAG
9 GEM	10 LEO	9 VIR	8 LIB	9 SAG	8 CAP
11 CAN	12 VIR	11 LIB	10 SCO	11 CAP	10 AQU
14 LEO	15 LIB	13 SCO	13 SAG	13 AQU	12 PIS
16 VIR	17 SCO	15 SAG	15 CAP	15 PIS	15 ARI
18 LIB	19 SAG	17 CAP	17 AQU	17 ARI	17 TAU
21 SCO	21 CAP	20 AQU	19 PIS	20 TAU	19 GEM
23 SAG	23 AQU	22 PIS	21 ARI	22 GEM	22 CAN
25 CAP	25 PIS	24 ARI	23 TAU	25 CAN	24 LEO
27 AQU	27 ARI	26 TAU	26 GEM	27 LEO	27 VIR
29 PIS	30 TAU	29 GEM	28 CAN	30 VIR	29 LIB
31 ARI			31 LEO		

1943

JUL	AUG	SEP	OCT	NOV	DEC
1 CAN	2 VIR	1 LIB	1 SCO	1 CAP	1 AQU
4 LEO	5 LIB	3 SCO	3 SAG	4 AQU	3 PIS
6 VIR	7 SCO	6 SAG	5 CAP	6 PIS	5 ARI
9 LIB	10 SAG	8 CAP	7 AQU	8 ARI	7 TAU
11 SCO	12 CAP	10 AQU	9 PIS	10 TAU	10 GEM
13 SAG	14 AQU	12 PIS	12 ARI	12 GEM	12 CAN
15 CAP	16 PIS	14 ARI	14 TAU	15 CAN	14 LEO
17 AQU	18 ARI	16 TAU	16 GEM	17 LEO	17 VIR
19 PIS	20 TAU	18 GEM	18 CAN	20 VIR	19 LIB
21 ARI	22 GEM	21 CAN	21 LEO	22 LIB	22 SCO
23 TAU	25 CAN	23 LEO	23 VIR	24 SCO	24 SAG
26 GEM	27 LEO	26 VIR	26 LIB	27 SAG	26 CAP
28 CAN	30 VIR	28 LIB	28 SCO	29 CAP	28 AQU
31 LEO			30 SAG		30 PIS

1944

JAN	FEB	MAR	APR	MAY	JUN
1 ARI	2 GEM	3 CAN	1 LEO	1 VIR	3 SCO
3 TAU	4 CAN	5 LEO	4 VIR	4 LIB	5 SAG
6 GEM	7 LEO	8 VIR	6 LIB	6 SCO	7 CAP
8 CAN	9 VIR	10 LIB	9 SCO	9 SAG	9 AQU
11 LEO	12 LIB	13 SCO	11 SAG	11 CAP	11 PIS
13 VIR	14 SCO	15 SAG	14 CAP	13 AQU	13 ARI
16 LIB	17 SAG	17 CAP	16 AQU	15 PIS	16 TAU
18 SCO	19 CAP	19 AQU	18 PIS	17 ARI	18 GEM
20 SAG	21 AQU	22 PIS	20 ARI	19 TAU	20 CAN
23 CAP	23 PIS	24 ARI	22 TAU	21 GEM	22 LEO
25 AQU	25 ARI	26 TAU	24 GEM	24 CAN	25 VIR
27 PIS	27 TAU	28 GEM	26 CAN	26 LEO	27 LIB
29 ARI	29 GEM	30 CAN	29 LEO	29 VIR	30 SCO
31 TAU				31 LIB	

1945

JAN	FEB	MAR	APR	MAY	JUN
2 VIR	1 LIB	3 SCO	1 SAG	1 CAP	2 PIS
4 LIB	3 SCO	5 SAG	4 CAP	3 AQU	4 ARI
7 SCO	6 SAG	8 CAP	6 AQU	6 PIS	6 TAU
9 SAG	8 CAP	10 AQU	8 PIS	8 ARI	8 GEM
12 CAP	10 AQU	12 PIS	10 ARI	10 TAU	10 CAN
14 AQU	12 PIS	14 ARI	12 TAU	12 GEM	12 LEO
16 PIS	14 ARI	16 TAU	14 GEM	14 CAN	15 VIR
18 ARI	17 TAU	18 GEM	16 CAN	16 LEO	17 LIB
20 TAU	19 GEM	20 CAN	19 LEO	18 VIR	20 SCO
22 GEM	21 CAN	22 LEO	21 VIR	21 LIB	22 SAG
25 CAN	23 LEO	25 VIR	24 LIB	23 SCO	25 CAP
27 LEO	26 VIR	27 LIB	26 SCO	26 SAG	27 AQU
29 VIR	28 LIB	30 SCO	29 SAG	28 CAP	29 PIS
				31 AQU	

1944

JUL	AUG	SEP	OCT	NOV	DEC
2 SAG	1 CAP	1 PIS	1 ARI	1 GEM	1 CAN
4 CAP	3 AQU	3 ARI	3 TAU	4 CAN	3 LEO
7 AQU	5 PIS	5 TAU	5 GEM	6 LEO	6 VIR
9 PIS	7 ARI	8 GEM	7 CAN	8 VIR	8 LIB
11 ARI	9 TAU	10 CAN	10 LEO	11 LIB	11 SCO
13 TAU	11 GEM	12 LEO	12 VIR	13 SCO	13 SAG
15 GEM	14 CAN	15 VIR	15 LIB	16 SAG	15 CAP
17 CAN	16 LEO	17 LIB	17 SCO	18 CAP	18 AQU
20 LEO	18 VIR	20 SCO	19 SAG	20 AQU	20 PIS
22 VIR	21 LIB	22 SAG	22 CAP	23 PIS	22 ARI
25 LIB	24 SCO	25 CAP	24 AQU	25 ARI	24 TAU
27 SCO	26 SAG	27 AQU	26 PIS	27 TAU	26 GEM
30 SAG	28 CAP	29 PIS	28 ARI	29 GEM	28 CAN
	30 AQU		30 TAU		31 LEO

1945

JUL	AUG	SEP	OCT	NOV	DEC
1 ARI	2 GEM	2 LEO	2 VIR	1 LIB	3 SAG
3 TAU	4 CAN	5 VIR	4 LIB	3 SCO	6 CAP
6 GEM	6 LEO	7 LIB	7 SCO	6 SAG	8 AQU
8 CAN	8 VIR	10 SCO	10 SAG	8 CAP	10 PIS
10 LEO	11 LIB	12 SAG	12 CAP	11 AQU	12 ARI
12 VIR	13 SCO	15 CAP	14 AQU	13 PIS	15 TAU
15 LIB	16 SAG	17 AQU	17 PIS	15 ARI	17 GEM
17 SCO	18 CAP	19 PIS	19 ARI	17 TAU	19 CAN
20 SAG	21 AQU	21 ARI	21 TAU	19 GEM	21 LEO
22 CAP	23 PIS	23 TAU	23 GEM	21 CAN	23 VIR
24 AQU	25 ARI	25 GEM	25 CAN	23 LEO	25 LIB
26 PIS	27 TAU	27 CAN	27 LEO	26 VIR	28 SCO
29 ARI	29 GEM	30 LEO	29 VIR	28 LIB	30 SAG
31 TAU	31 CAN			30 SCO	

1946

JAN	FEB	MAR	APR	MAY	JUN
2 CAP	1 AQU	2 PIS	1 ARI	2 GEM	1 CAN
4 AQU	3 PIS	4 ARI	3 TAU	4 CAN	3 LEO
6 PIS	5 ARI	6 TAU	5 GEM	6 LEO	5 VIR
9 ARI	7 TAU	8 GEM	7 CAN	8 VIR	7 LIB
11 TAU	9 GEM	11 CAN	9 LEO	11 LIB	10 SCO
13 GEM	11 CAN	13 LEO	11 VIR	13 SCO	12 SAG
15 CAN	13 LEO	15 VIR	14 LIB	16 SAG	15 CAP
17 LEO	16 VIR	17 LIB	16 SCO	18 CAP	17 AQU
19 VIR	18 LIB	20 SCO	19 SAG	21 AQU	20 PIS
22 LIB	20 SCO	22 SAG	21 CAP	23 PIS	22 ARI
24 SCO	23 SAG	25 CAP	24 AQU	26 ARI	24 TAU
27 SAG	26 CAP	27 AQU	26 PIS	28 TAU	26 GEM
29 CAP	28 AQU	30 PIS	28 ARI	30 GEM	28 CAN
			30 TAU		30 LEO

1947

JAN	FEB	MAR	APR	MAY	JUN
1 TAU	2 CAN	1 CAN	2 VIR	1 LIB	2 SAG
3 GEM	4 LEO	3 LEO	4 LIB	3 SCO	5 CAP
5 CAN	6 VIR	5 VIR	6 SCO	6 SAG	7 AQU
7 LEO	8 LIB	7 LIB	8 SAG	8 CAP	10 PIS
9 VIR	10 SCO	10 SCO	11 CAP	11 AQU	12 ARI
12 LIB	13 SAG	12 SAG	13 AQU	13 PIS	14 TAU
14 SCO	15 CAP	15 CAP	16 PIS	16 ARI	16 GEM
16 SAG	18 AQU	17 AQU	18 ARI	18 TAU	18 CAN
19 CAP	20 PIS	20 PIS	20 TAU	20 GEM	20 LEO
22 AQU	23 ARI	22 ARI	23 GEM	22 CAN	22 VIR
24 PIS	25 TAU	24 TAU	25 CAN	24 LEO	25 LIB
26 ARI	27 GEM	26 GEM	27 LEO	26 VIR	27 SCO
29 TAU		28 CAN	29 VIR	28 LIB	29 SAG
31 GEM		31 LEO		31 SCO	

1946

JUL	AUG	SEP	OCT	NOV	DEC
2 VIR	1 LIB	2 SAG	2 CAP	1 AQU	3 ARI
4 LIB	3 SCO	5 CAP	4 AQU	3 PIS	5 TAU
7 SCO	6 SAG	7 AQU	7 PIS	5 ARI	7 GEM
9 SAG	8 CAP	9 PIS	9 ARI	7 TAU	9 CAN
12 CAP	11 AQU	12 ARI	11 TAU	10 GEM	11 LEO
14 AQU	13 PIS	14 TAU	13 GEM	12 CAN	13 VIR
17 PIS	15 ARI	16 GEM	15 CAN	14 LEO	15 LIB
19 ARI	17 TAU	18 CAN	17 LEO	16 VIR	18 SCO
21 TAU	20 GEM	20 LEO	20 VIR	18 LIB	20 SAG
23 GEM	22 CAN	22 VIR	22 LIB	20 SCO	23 CAP
25 CAN	24 LEO	25 LIB	24 SCO	23 SAG	25 AQU
27 LEO	26 VIR	27 SCO	27 SAG	25 CAP	28 PIS
30 VIR	28 LIB	29 SAG	29 CAP	28 AQU	30 ARI
	31 SCO			30 PIS	

1947

JUL	AUG	SEP	OCT	NOV	DEC
2 CAP	1 AQU	2 ARI	1 TAU	2 CAN	1 LEO
4 AQU	3 PIS	4 TAU	4 GEM	4 LEO	3 VIR
7 PIS	6 ARI	6 GEM	6 CAN	6 VIR	6 LIB
9 ARI	8 TAU	9 CAN	8 LEO	8 LIB	8 SCO
12 TAU	10 GEM	11 LEO	10 VIR	11 SCO	10 SAG
14 GEM	12 CAN	13 VIR	12 LIB	13 SAG	13 CAP
16 CAN	14 LEO	15 LIB	14 SCO	15 CAP	15 AQU
18 LEO	16 VIR	17 SCO	17 SAG	18 AQU	18 PIS
20 VIR	18 LIB	19 SAG	19 CAP	20 PIS	20 ARI
22 LIB	20 SCO	22 CAP	22 AQU	23 ARI	23 TAU
24 SCO	23 SAG	24 AQU	24 PIS	25 TAU	25 GEM
27 SAG	25 CAP	27 PIS	26 ARI	27 GEM	27 CAN
29 CAP	28 AQU	29 ARI	29 TAU	29 CAN	29 LEO
	30 PIS		31 GEM		31 VIR

1948

JAN	FEB	MAR	APR	MAY	JUN
2 LIB	3 SAG	1 SAG	2 AQU	2 PIS	1 ARI
4 SCO	5 CAP	3 CAP	5 PIS	5 ARI	3 TAU
6 SAG	8 AQU	6 AQU	7 ARI	7 TAU	6 GEM
9 CAP	10 PIS	8 PIS	10 TAU	9 GEM	8 CAN
11 AQU	13 ARI	11 ARI	12 GEM	11 CAN	10 LEO
14 PIS	15 TAU	13 TAU	14 CAN	14 LEO	12 VIR
16 ARI	17 GEM	16 GEM	16 LEO	16 VIR	14 LIB
19 TAU	20 CAN	18 CAN	18 VIR	18 LIB	16 SCO
21 GEM	22 LEO	20 LEO	21 LIB	20 SCO	18 SAG
23 CAN	24 VIR	22 VIR	23 SCO	22 SAG	21 CAP
25 LEO	26 LIB	24 LIB	25 SAG	25 CAP	23 AQU
27 VIR	28 SCO	26 SCO	27 CAP	27 AQU	26 PIS
29 LIB		28 SAG	30 AQU	29 PIS	28 ARI
31 SCO		31 CAP			

1949

JAN	FEB	MAR	APR	MAY	JUN
3 PIS	2 ARI	1 ARI	2 GEM	2 CAN	2 VIR
5 ARI	4 TAU	3 TAU	5 CAN	4 LEO	5 LIB
8 TAU	7 GEM	6 GEM	7 LEO	6 VIR	7 SCO
10 GEM	9 CAN	8 CAN	9 VIR	8 LIB	9 SAG
12 CAN	11 LEO	10 LEO	11 LIB	10 SCO	11 CAP
15 LEO	13 VIR	13 VIR	13 SCO	12 SAG	13 AQU
17 VIR	15 LIB	15 LIB	15 SAG	15 CAP	16 PIS
19 LIB	17 SCO	17 SCO	17 CAP	17 AQU	18 ARI
21 SCO	19 SAG	19 SAG	19 AQU	19 PIS	21 TAU
23 SAG	22 CAP	21 CAP	22 PIS	22 ARI	23 GEM
25 CAP	24 AQU	23 AQU	24 ARI	24 TAU	25 CAN
28 AQU	26 PIS	26 PIS	27 TAU	27 GEM	28 LEO
30 PIS		28 ARI	29 GEM	29 CAN	30 VIR
		31 TAU		31 LEO	

1948

JUL	AUG	SEP	OCT	NOV	DEC
1 TAU	2 CAN	2 VIR	1 LIB	2 SAG	2 CAP
3 GEM	4 LEO	4 LIB	3 SCO	4 CAP	4 AQU
5 CAN	6 VIR	6 SCO	6 SAG	7 AQU	6 PIS
7 LEO	8 LIB	8 SAG	8 CAP	9 PIS	9 ARI
9 VIR	10 SCO	11 CAP	10 AQU	12 ARI	12 TAU
11 LIB	12 SAG	13 AQU	13 PIS	14 TAU	14 GEM
13 SCO	14 CAP	16 PIS	15 ARI	17 GEM	16 CAN
16 SAG	17 AQU	18 ARI	18 TAU	19 CAN	18 LEO
18 CAP	19 PIS	21 TAU	20 GEM	21 LEO	20 VIR
21 AQU	22 ARI	23 GEM	23 CAN	23 VIR	22 LIB
23 PIS	24 TAU	25 CAN	25 LEO	25 LIB	25 SCO
26 ARI	27 GEM	27 LEO	27 VIR	27 SCO	27 SAG
28 TAU	29 CAN	29 VIR	29 LIB	29 SAG	29 CAP
30 GEM	31 LEO		31 SCO		31 AQU

1949

JUL	AUG	SEP	OCT	NOV	DEC
2 LIB	2 SAG	1 CAP	3 PIS	2 ARI	1 TAU
4 SCO	5 CAP	3 AQU	5 ARI	4 TAU	4 GEM
6 SAG	7 AQU	6 PIS	8 TAU	7 GEM	6 CAN
8 CAP	9 PIS	8 ARI	10 GEM	9 CAN	9 LEO
11 AQU	12 ARI	11 TAU	13 CAN	11 LEO	11 VIR
13 PIS	14 TAU	13 GEM	15 LEO	14 VIR	13 LIB
15 ARI	17 GEM	15 CAN	17 VIR	16 LIB	15 SCO
18 TAU	19 CAN	18 LEO	19 LIB	18 SCO	17 SAG
20 GEM	21 LEO	20 VIR	21 SCO	20 SAG	19 CAP
23 CAN	23 VIR	22 LIB	23 SAG	22 CAP	21 AQU
25 LEO	25 LIB	24 SCO	25 CAP	24 AQU	24 PIS
27 VIR	27 SCO	26 SAG	28 AQU	26 PIS	26 ARI
29 LIB	30 SAG	28 CAP	30 PIS	29 ARI	29 TAU
31 SCO		30 AQU			31 GEM

1950

JAN	FEB	MAR	APR	MAY	JUN
3 CAN	1 LEO	1 LEO	1 LIB	1 SCO	1 CAP
5 LEO	3 VIR	3 VIR	3 SCO	3 SAG	3 AQU
7 VIR	6 LIB	5 LIB	5 SAG	5 CAP	5 PIS
9 LIB	8 SCO	7 SCO	7 CAP	7 AQU	8 ARI
11 SCO	10 SAG	9 SAG	10 AQU	9 PIS	10 TAU
14 SAG	12 CAP	11 CAP	12 PIS	12 ARI	13 GEM
16 CAP	14 AQU	13 AQU	14 ARI	14 TAU	15 CAN
18 AQU	16 PIS	16 PIS	17 TAU	17 GEM	18 LEO
20 PIS	19 ARI	18 ARI	19 GEM	19 CAN	20 VIR
22 ARI	21 TAU	21 TAU	22 CAN	22 LEO	22 LIB
25 TAU	24 GEM	23 GEM	24 LEO	24 VIR	25 SCO
28 GEM	26 CAN	26 CAN	27 VIR	26 LIB	27 SAG
30 CAN		28 LEO	29 LIB	28 SCO	29 CAP
		30 VIR		30 SAG	

1951

JAN	FEB	MAR	APR	MAY	JUN
2 SCO	2 CAP	2 CAP	2 PIS	2 ARI	3 GEM
4 SAG	4 AQU	4 AQU	5 ARI	4 TAU	5 CAN
6 CAP	7 PIS	6 PIS	7 TAU	7 GEM	8 LEO
8 AQU	9 ARI	8 ARI	9 GEM	9 CAN	10 VIR
10 PIS	11 TAU	11 TAU	12 CAN	12 LEO	13 LIB
12 ARI	14 GEM	13 GEM	14 LEO	14 VIR	15 SCO
15 TAU	16 CAN	16 CAN	17 VIR	16 LIB	17 SAG
17 GEM	19 LEO	18 LEO	19 LIB	19 SCO	19 CAP
20 CAN	21 VIR	20 VIR	21 SCO	21 SAG	21 AQU
22 LEO	23 LIB	23 LIB	23 SAG	23 CAP	23 PIS
25 VIR	25 SCO	25 SCO	25 CAP	25 AQU	25 ARI
27 LIB	28 SAG	27 SAG	27 AQU	27 PIS	28 TAU
29 SCO		29 CAP	29 PIS	29 ARI	30 GEM
31 SAG		31 AQU		31 TAU	

1950

JUL	AUG	SEP	OCT	NOV	DEC
1 AQU	2 ARI	3 GEM	3 CAN	2 LEO	1 VIR
3 PIS	4 TAU	5 CAN	5 LEO	4 VIR	3 LIB
5 ARI	7 GEM	8 LEO	7 VIR	6 LIB	6 SCO
8 TAU	9 CAN	10 VIR	10 LIB	8 SCO	8 SAG
10 GEM	11 LEO	12 LIB	12 SCO	10 SAG	10 CAP
13 CAN	14 VIR	14 SCO	14 SAG	12 CAP	12 AQU
15 LEO	16 LIB	16 SAG	16 CAP	14 AQU	14 PIS
17 VIR	18 SCO	18 CAP	18 AQU	16 PIS	16 ARI
20 LIB	20 SAG	21 AQU	20 PIS	19 ARI	19 TAU
22 SCO	22 CAP	23 PIS	23 ARI	21 TAU	21 GEM
24 SAG	24 AQU	25 ARI	25 TAU	24 GEM	24 CAN
26 CAP	27 PIS	28 TAU	28 GEM	26 CAN	26 LEO
28 AQU	29 ARI	30 GEM	30 CAN	29 LEO	28 VIR
30 PIS	31 TAU				31 LIB

1951

JUL	AUG	SEP	OCT	NOV	DEC
3 CAN	1 LEO	3 LIB	2 SCO	1 SAG	2 AQU
5 LEO	4 VIR	5 SCO	4 SAG	3 CAP	4 PIS
8 VIR	6 LIB	7 SAG	6 CAP	5 AQU	6 ARI
10 LIB	9 SCO	9 CAP	8 AQU	7 PIS	9 TAU
12 SCO	11 SAG	11 AQU	11 PIS	9 ARI	11 GEM
14 SAG	13 CAP	13 PIS	13 ARI	11 TAU	13 CAN
16 CAP	15 AQU	15 ARI	15 TAU	14 GEM	16 LEO
18 AQU	17 PIS	18 TAU	17 GEM	16 CAN	19 VIR
20 PIS	19 ARI	20 GEM	20 CAN	19 LEO	21 LIB
23 ARI	21 TAU	23 CAN	22 LEO	21 VIR	23 SCO
25 TAU	24 GEM	25 LEO	25 VIR	24 LIB	25 SAG
27 GEM	26 CAN	28 VIR	27 LIB	26 SCO	27 CAP
30 CAN	29 LEO	30 LIB	29 SCO	28 SAG	29 AQU
	31 VIR			30 CAP	31 PIS

1952

JAN	FEB	MAR	APR	MAY	JUN
3 ARI	1 TAU	2 GEM	1 CAN	3 VIR	2 LIB
5 TAU	3 GEM	4 CAN	3 LEO	5 LIB	4 SCO
7 GEM	6 CAN	7 LEO	6 VIR	8 SCO	6 SAG
10 CAN	9 LEO	9 VIR	8 LIB	10 SAG	8 CAP
12 LEO	11 VIR	12 LIB	10 SCO	12 CAP	10 AQU
15 VIR	14 LIB	14 SCO	13 SAG	14 AQU	12 PIS
17 LIB	16 SCO	16 SAG	15 CAP	16 PIS	15 ARI
20 SCO	18 SAG	19 CAP	17 AQU	18 ARI	17 TAU
22 SAG	20 CAP	21 AQU	19 PIS	21 TAU	19 GEM
24 CAP	22 AQU	23 PIS	21 ARI	23 GEM	22 CAN
26 AQU	24 PIS	25 ARI	23 TAU	25 CAN	24 LEO
28 PIS	26 ARI	27 TAU	26 GEM	28 LEO	27 VIR
30 ARI	29 TAU	29 GEM	28 CAN	30 VIR	29 LIB
			30 LEO		

1953

JAN	FEB	MAR	APR	MAY	JUN
1 LEO	3 LIB	2 LIB	1 SCO	2 CAP	1 AQU
4 VIR	5 SCO	4 SCO	3 SAG	5 AQU	3 PIS
6 LIB	7 SAG	7 SAG	5 CAP	7 PIS	5 ARI
9 SCO	10 CAP	9 CAP	7 AQU	9 ARI	7 TAU
11 SAG	12 AQU	11 AQU	10 PIS	11 TAU	9 GEM
13 CAP	14 PIS	13 PIS	12 ARI	13 GEM	12 CAN
15 AQU	16 ARI	15 ARI	14 TAU	15 CAN	14 LEO
17 PIS	18 TAU	17 TAU	16 GEM	18 LEO	16 VIR
19 ARI	20 GEM	19 GEM	18 CAN	20 VIR	19 LIB
21 TAU	22 CAN	22 CAN	20 LEO	23 LIB	21 SCO
24 GEM	25 LEO	24 LEO	23 VIR	25 SCO	24 SAG
26 CAN	27 VIR	27 VIR	25 LIB	27 SAG	26 CAP
28 LEO		29 LIB	28 SCO	30 CAP	28 AQU
31 VIR			30 SAG		30 PIS

1952

JUL	AUG	SEP	OCT	NOV	DEC
2 SCO	2 CAP	1 AQU	2 ARI	1 TAU	2 CAN
4 SAG	4 AQU	3 PIS	4 TAU	3 GEM	5 LEO
6 CAP	6 PIS	5 ARI	6 GEM	5 CAN	7 VIR
8 AQU	8 ARI	7 TAU	9 CAN	7 LEO	10 LIB
10 PIS	10 TAU	9 GEM	11 LEO	10 VIR	12 SCO
12 ARI	13 GEM	11 CAN	14 VIR	13 LIB	15 SAG
14 TAU	15 CAN	14 LEO	16 LIB	15 SCO	17 CAP
16 GEM	18 LEO	16 VIR	19 SCO	17 SAG	19 AQU
19 CAN	20 VIR	19 LIB	21 SAG	19 CAP	21 PIS
21 LEO	23 LIB	21 SCO	23 CAP	21 AQU	23 ARI
24 VIR	25 SCO	24 SAG	25 AQU	24 PIS	25 TAU
26 LIB	27 SAG	26 CAP	27 PIS	26 ARI	27 GEM
29 SCO	30 CAP	28 AQU	29 ARI	28 TAU	30 CAN
31 SAG		30 PIS		30 GEM	

1953

JUL	AUG	SEP	OCT	NOV	DEC
2 ARI	1 TAU	1 CAN	1 LEO	2 LIB	2 SCO
5 TAU	3 GEM	4 LEO	4 VIR	5 SCO	5 SAG
7 GEM	5 CAN	6 VIR	6 LIB	7 SAG	7 CAP
9 CAN	8 LEO	9 LIB	9 SCO	10 CAP	9 AQU
11 LEO	10 VIR	11 SCO	11 SAG	12 AQU	11 PIS
14 VIR	13 LIB	14 SAG	13 CAP	14 PIS	14 ARI
16 LIB	15 SCO	16 CAP	16 AQU	16 ARI	16 TAU
19 SCO	18 SAG	18 AQU	18 PIS	18 TAU	18 GEM
21 SAG	20 CAP	21 PIS	20 ARI	20 GEM	20 CAN
23 CAP	22 AQU	23 ARI	22 TAU	22 CAN	22 LEO
26 AQU	24 PIS	25 TAU	24 GEM	25 LEO	25 VIR
28 PIS	26 ARI	27 GEM	26 CAN	27 VIR	27 LIB
30 ARI	28 TAU	29 CAN	28 LEO	30 LIB	30 SCO
	30 GEM		31 VIR		

1954

JAN	FEB	MAR	APR	MAY	JUN
1 SAG	2 AQU	1 AQU	2 ARI	1 TAU	2 CAN
3 CAP	4 PIS	3 PIS	4 TAU	3 GEM	4 LEO
6 AQU	6 ARI	5 ARI	6 GEM	5 CAN	6 VIR
8 PIS	8 TAU	7 TAU	8 CAN	8 LEO	9 LIB
10 ARI	10 GEM	10 GEM	10 LEO	10 VIR	11 SCO
12 TAU	13 CAN	12 CAN	13 VIR	12 LIB	14 SAG
14 GEM	15 LEO	14 LEO	15 LIB	15 SCO	16 CAP
16 CAN	17 VIR	16 VIR	18 SCO	17 SAG	19 AQU
19 LEO	20 LIB	19 LIB	20 SAG	20 CAP	21 PIS
21 VIR	22 SCO	21 SCO	23 CAP	22 AQU	23 ARI
23 LIB	25 SAG	24 SAG	25 AQU	25 PIS	25 TAU
26 SCO	27 CAP	26 CAP	27 PIS	27 ARI	27 GEM
28 SAG		29 AQU	29 ARI	29 TAU	29 CAN
31 CAP		31 PIS		31 GEM	

1955

JAN	FEB	MAR	APR	MAY	JUN
3 TAU	1 GEM	2 CAN	1 LEO	2 LIB	1 SCO
5 GEM	3 CAN	4 LEO	3 VIR	5 SCO	4 SAG
7 CAN	5 LEO	7 VIR	5 LIB	7 SAG	6 CAP
9 LEO	7 VIR	9 LIB	8 SCO	10 CAP	9 AQU
11 VIR	10 LIB	11 SCO	10 SAG	12 AQU	11 PIS
13 LIB	12 SCO	14 SAG	13 CAP	15 PIS	13 ARI
16 SCO	15 SAG	16 CAP	15 AQU	17 ARI	16 TAU
18 SAG	17 CAP	19 AQU	18 PIS	19 TAU	18 GEM
21 CAP	19 AQU	21 PIS	20 ARI	21 GEM	20 CAN
23 AQU	22 PIS	23 ARI	22 TAU	23 CAN	22 LEO
25 PIS	24 ARI	25 TAU	24 GEM	25 LEO	24 VIR
28 ARI	26 TAU	27 GEM	26 CAN	27 VIR	26 LIB
30 TAU	28 GEM	29 CAN	28 LEO	30 LIB	28 SCO
			30 VIR		

1954

JUL	AUG	SEP	OCT	NOV	DEC
1 LEO	2 LIB	1 SCO	1 SAG	2 AQU	2 PIS
4 VIR	5 SCO	4 SAG	4 CAP	5 PIS	4 ARI
6 LIB	7 SAG	6 CAP	6 AQU	7 ARI	6 TAU
9 SCO	10 CAP	9 AQU	8 PIS	9 TAU	8 GEM
11 SAG	12 AQU	11 PIS	10 ARI	11 GEM	10 CAN
14 CAP	14 PIS	13 ARI	12 TAU	13 CAN	12 LEO
16 AQU	16 ARI	15 TAU	14 GEM	15 LEO	14 VIR
18 PIS	19 TAU	17 GEM	16 CAN	17 VIR	17 LIB
20 ARI	21 GEM	19 CAN	19 LEO	20 LIB	19 SCO
22 TAU	23 CAN	21 LEO	21 VIR	22 SCO	22 SAG
24 GEM	25 LEO	24 VIR	23 LIB	25 SAG	24 CAP
27 CAN	27 VIR	26 LIB	26 SCO	27 CAP	27 AQU
29 LEO	30 LIB	29 SCO	28 SAG	30 AQU	29 PIS
31 VIR			31 CAP		31 ARI

1955

JUL	AUG	SEP	OCT	NOV	DEC
1 SAG	2 AQU	1 PIS	1 ARI	1 GEM	1 CAN
3 CAP	5 PIS	3 ARI	3 TAU	3 CAN	3 LEO
6 AQU	7 ARI	5 TAU	5 GEM	5 LEO	5 VIR
8 PIS	9 TAU	8 GEM	7 CAN	7 VIR	7 LIB
11 ARI	11 GEM	10 CAN	9 LEO	10 LIB	9 SCO
13 TAU	13 CAN	12 LEO	11 VIR	12 SCO	12 SAG
15 GEM	15 LEO	14 VIR	13 LIB	15 SAG	14 CAP
17 CAN	18 VIR	16 LIB	16 SCO	17 CAP	17 AQU
19 LEO	20 LIB	18 SCO	18 SAG	20 AQU	19 PIS
21 VIR	22 SCO	21 SAG	21 CAP	22 PIS	22 ARI
23 LIB	25 SAG	23 CAP	23 AQU	24 ARI	24 TAU
26 SCO	27 CAP	26 AQU	26 PIS	27 TAU	26 GEM
28 SAG	30 AQU	28 PIS	28 ARI	29 GEM	28 CAN
31 CAP			30 TAU		30 LEO

1956

JAN	FEB	MAR	APR	MAY	JUN
1 VIR	2 SCO	3 SAG	1 CAP	1 AQU	3 ARI
3 LIB	4 SAG	5 CAP	4 AQU	4 PIS	5 TAU
6 SCO	7 CAP	8 AQU	6 PIS	6 ARI	7 GEM
8 SAG	9 AQU	10 PIS	9 ARI	8 TAU	9 CAN
11 CAP	12 PIS	12 ARI	11 TAU	11 GEM	11 LEO
13 AQU	14 ARI	15 TAU	13 GEM	13 CAN	13 VIR
16 PIS	16 TAU	17 GEM	15 CAN	15 LEO	15 LIB
18 ARI	19 GEM	19 CAN	17 LEO	17 VIR	18 SCO
20 TAU	21 CAN	21 LEO	20 VIR	19 LIB	20 SAG
22 GEM	23 LEO	23 VIR	22 LIB	21 SCO	22 CAP
24 CAN	25 VIR	25 LIB	24 SCO	24 SAG	25 AQU
26 LEO	27 LIB	28 SCO	26 SAG	26 CAP	27 PIS
28 VIR	29 SCO	30 SAG	29 CAP	29 AQU	30 ARI
31 LIB				31 PIS	

1957

JAN	FEB	MAR	APR	MAY	JUN
2 AQU	1 PIS	3 ARI	1 TAU	1 GEM	1 LEO
5 PIS	3 ARI	5 TAU	4 GEM	3 CAN	4 VIR
7 ARI	6 TAU	7 GEM	6 CAN	5 LEO	6 LIB
9 TAU	8 GEM	10 CAN	8 LEO	7 VIR	8 SCO
12 GEM	10 CAN	12 LEO	10 VIR	9 LIB	10 SAG
14 CAN	12 LEO	14 VIR	12 LIB	12 SCO	12 CAP
16 LEO	14 VIR	16 LIB	14 SCO	14 SAG	15 AQU
18 VIR	16 LIB	18 SCO	16 SAG	16 CAP	17 PIS
20 LIB	18 SCO	20 SAG	19 CAP	18 AQU	20 ARI
22 SCO	21 SAG	22 CAP	21 AQU	21 PIS	22 TAU
24 SAG	23 CAP	25 AQU	24 PIS	23 ARI	25 GEM
27 CAP	26 AQU	27 PIS	26 ARI	26 TAU	27 CAN
29 AQU	28 PIS	30 ARI	29 TAU	28 GEM	29 LEO
				30 CAN	

1956

JUL	AUG	SEP	OCT	NOV	DEC
2 TAU	1 GEM	1 LEO	1 VIR	1 SCO	1 SAG
4 GEM	3 CAN	3 VIR	3 LIB	3 SAG	3 CAP
6 CAN	5 LEO	5 LIB	5 SCO	6 CAP	6 AQU
8 LEO	7 VIR	7 SCO	7 SAG	8 AQU	8 PIS
10 VIR	9 LIB	10 SAG	10 CAP	11 PIS	11 ARI
12 LIB	11 SCO	12 CAP	12 AQU	13 ARI	13 TAU
15 SCO	13 SAG	15 AQU	15 PIS	16 TAU	15 GEM
17 SAG	16 CAP	17 PIS	17 ARI	18 GEM	17 CAN
20 CAP	18 AQU	20 ARI	19 TAU	20 CAN	19 LEO
22 AQU	21 PIS	22 TAU	22 GEM	22 LEO	21 VIR
25 PIS	23 ARI	24 GEM	24 CAN	24 VIR	24 LIB
27 ARI	26 TAU	26 CAN	26 LEO	26 LIB	26 SCO
30 TAU	28 GEM	29 LEO	28 VIR	29 SCO	28 SAG
	30 CAN		30 LIB		31 CAP

1957

JUL	AUG	SEP	OCT	NOV	DEC
1 VIR	1 SCO	2 CAP	2 AQU	1 PIS	1 ARI
3 LIB	4 SAG	5 AQU	4 PIS	3 ARI	3 TAU
5 SCO	6 CAP	7 PIS	7 ARI	6 TAU	5 GEM
7 SAG	8 AQU	10 ARI	9 TAU	8 GEM	8 CAN
10 CAP	11 PIS	12 TAU	12 GEM	10 CAN	10 LEO
12 AQU	13 ARI	15 GEM	14 CAN	13 LEO	12 VIR
15 PIS	16 TAU	17 CAN	16 LEO	15 VIR	14 LIB
17 ARI	18 GEM	19 LEO	18 VIR	17 LIB	16 SCO
20 TAU	21 CAN	21 VIR	21 LIB	19 SCO	18 SAG
22 GEM	23 LEO	23 LIB	23 SCO	21 SAG	21 CAP
24 CAN	25 VIR	25 SCO	25 SAG	23 CAP	23 AQU
26 LEO	27 LIB	27 SAG	27 CAP	26 AQU	25 PIS
28 VIR	29 SCO	29 CAP	29 AQU	28 PIS	28 ARI
30 LIB	31 SAG				30 TAU

1958

JAN	FEB	MAR	APR	MAY	JUN
2 GEM	3 LEO	2 LEO	1 VIR	2 SCO	3 CAP
4 CAN	5 VIR	4 VIR	3 LIB	4 SAG	5 AQU
6 LEO	7 LIB	6 LIB	5 SCO	6 CAP	7 PIS
8 VIR	9 SCO	8 SCO	7 SAG	8 AQU	10 ARI
10 LIB	11 SAG	10 SAG	9 CAP	11 PIS	12 TAU
12 SCO	13 CAP	12 CAP	11 AQU	13 ARI	15 GEM
15 SAG	16 AQU	15 AQU	13 PIS	16 TAU	17 CAN
17 CAP	18 PIS	17 PIS	16 ARI	18 GEM	19 LEO
19 AQU	21 ARI	20 ARI	19 TAU	21 CAN	21 VIR
22 PIS	23 TAU	22 TAU	21 GEM	23 LEO	24 LIB
24 ARI	26 GEM	25 GEM	23 CAN	25 VIR	26 SCO
27 TAU	28 CAN	27 CAN	26 LEO	27 LIB	28 SAG
29 GEM		29 LEO	28 VIR	29 SCO	30 CAP
31 CAN			30 LIB	31 SAG	

1959

JAN	FEB	MAR	APR	MAY	JUN
1 LIB	1 SAG	1 SAG	1 AQU	1 PIS	2 TAU
3 SCO	4 CAP	3 CAP	4 PIS	3 ARI	5 GEM
5 SAG	6 AQU	5 AQU	6 ARI	6 TAU	7 CAN
7 CAP	8 PIS	7 PIS	8 TAU	8 GEM	9 LEO
9 AQU	10 ARI	10 ARI	11 GEM	11 CAN	12 VIR
12 PIS	13 TAU	12 TAU	14 CAN	13 LEO	14 LIB
14 ARI	15 GEM	15 GEM	16 LEO	16 VIR	16 SCO
17 TAU	18 CAN	17 CAN	18 VIR	18 LIB	18 SAG
19 GEM	20 LEO	20 LEO	20 LIB	20 SCO	20 CAP
21 CAN	22 VIR	22 VIR	22 SCO	22 SAG	22 AQU
24 LEO	24 LIB	24 LIB	24 SAG	24 CAP	24 PIS
26 VIR	27 SCO	26 SCO	26 CAP	26 AQU	27 ARI
28 LIB		28 SAG	28 AQU	28 PIS	29 TAU
30 SCO		30 CAP		30 ARI	

1958

JUL	AUG	SEP	OCT	NOV	DEC
2 AQU	1 PIS	2 TAU	2 GEM	1 CAN	3 VIR
4 PIS	3 ARI	5 GEM	4 CAN	3 LEO	5 LIB
7 ARI	6 TAU	7 CAN	7 LEO	5 VIR	7 SCO
9 TAU	8 GEM	9 LEO	9 VIR	7 LIB	9 SAG
12 GEM	11 CAN	11 VIR	11 LIB	9 SCO	11 CAP
14 CAN	13 LEO	13 LIB	13 SCO	11 SAG	13 AQU
17 LEO	15 VIR	15 SCO	15 SAG	13 CAP	15 PIS
19 VIR	17 LIB	18 SAG	17 CAP	16 AQU	18 ARI
21 LIB	19 SCO	20 CAP	19 AQU	18 PIS	20 TAU
23 SCO	21 SAG	22 AQU	22 PIS	20 ARI	23 GEM
25 SAG	23 CAP	24 PIS	24 ARI	23 TAU	25 CAN
27 CAP	26 AQU	27 ARI	27 TAU	25 GEM	27 LEO
29 AQU	28 PIS	29 TAU	29 GEM	28 CAN	30 VIR
	31 ARI			30 LEO	

1959

JUL	AUG	SEP	OCT	NOV	DEC
2 GEM	1 CAN	2 VIR	1 LIB	2 SAG	1 CAP
4 CAN	3 LEO	4 LIB	3 SCO	4 CAP	3 AQU
7 LEO	5 VIR	6 SCO	5 SAG	6 AQU	5 PIS
9 VIR	8 LIB	8 SAG	7 CAP	8 PIS	8 ARI
11 LIB	10 SCO	10 CAP	10 AQU	10 ARI	10 TAU
13 SCO	12 SAG	12 AQU	12 PIS	13 TAU	13 GEM
16 SAG	14 CAP	15 PIS	14 ARI	15 GEM	15 CAN
18 CAP	16 AQU	17 ARI	17 TAU	18 CAN	18 LEO
20 AQU	18 PIS	19 TAU	19 GEM	20 LEO	20 VIR
22 PIS	20 ARI	22 GEM	22 CAN	23 VIR	22 LIB
24 ARI	23 TAU	24 CAN	24 LEO	25 LIB	25 SCO
27 TAU	25 GEM	27 LEO	26 VIR	27 SCO	27 SAG
29 GEM	28 CAN	29 VIR	29 LIB	29 SAG	29 CAP
	30 LEO		31 SCO		31 AQU

1960

JAN	FEB	MAR	APR	MAY	JUN
2 PIS	3 TAU	1 TAU	2 CAN	2 LEO	1 VIR
4 ARI	5 GEM	4 GEM	5 LEO	5 VIR	3 LIB
6 TAU	8 CAN	6 CAN	7 VIR	7 LIB	6 SCO
9 GEM	10 LEO	9 LEO	10 LIB	9 SCO	8 SAG
11 CAN	13 VIR	11 VIR	12 SCO	11 SAG	10 CAP
14 LEO	15 LIB	13 LIB	14 SAG	13 CAP	12 AQU
16 VIR	17 SCO	15 SCO	16 CAP	15 AQU	14 PIS
19 LIB	19 SAG	17 SAG	18 AQU	17 PIS	16 ARI
21 SCO	21 CAP	20 CAP	20 PIS	20 ARI	18 TAU
23 SAG	23 AQU	22 AQU	22 ARI	22 TAU	21 GEM
25 CAP	26 PIS	24 PIS	25 TAU	24 GEM	23 CAN
27 AQU	28 ARI	26 ARI	27 GEM	27 CAN	26 LEO
29 PIS		28 TAU	30 CAN	29 LEO	28 VIR
31 ARI		31 GEM			

1961

JAN	FEB	MAR	APR	MAY	JUN
3 LEO	2 VIR	1 VIR	2 SCO	2 SAG	2 AQU
5 VIR	4 LIB	3 LIB	4 SAG	4 CAP	4 PIS
8 LIB	6 SCO	6 SCO	6 CAP	6 AQU	6 ARI
10 SCO	9 SAG	8 SAG	9 AQU	8 PIS	8 TAU
12 SAG	11 CAP	10 CAP	11 PIS	10 ARI	11 GEM
14 CAP	13 AQU	12 AQU	13 ARI	12 TAU	13 CAN
16 AQU	15 PIS	14 PIS	15 TAU	14 GEM	16 LEO
18 PIS	17 ARI	16 ARI	17 GEM	17 CAN	18 VIR
20 ARI	19 TAU	18 TAU	19 CAN	19 LEO	21 LIB
23 TAU	21 GEM	21 GEM	22 LEO	22 VIR	23 SCO
25 GEM	24 CAN	23 CAN	25 VIR	24 LIB	25 SAG
28 CAN	26 LEO	26 LEO	27 LIB	27 SCO	27 CAP
30 LEO		28 VIR	29 SCO	29 SAG	29 AQU
		31 LIB		31 CAP	

1960

JUL	AUG	SEP	OCT	NOV	DEC
1 LIB	1 SAG	2 AQU	1 PIS	2 TAU	2 GEM
3 SCO	3 CAP	4 PIS	3 ARI	4 GEM	4 CAN
5 SAG	5 AQU	6 ARI	6 TAU	7 CAN	7 LEO
7 CAP	7 PIS	8 TAU	8 GEM	9 LEO	9 VIR
9 AQU	10 ARI	11 GEM	10 CAN	12 VIR	12 LIB
11 PIS	12 TAU	13 CAN	13 LEO	14 LIB	14 SCO
13 ARI	14 GEM	16 LEO	15 VIR	16 SCO	16 SAG
15 TAU	17 CAN	18 VIR	18 LIB	19 SAG	18 CAP
18 GEM	19 LEO	20 LIB	20 SCO	21 CAP	20 AQU
20 CAN	22 VIR	23 SCO	22 SAG	23 AQU	22 PIS
23 LEO	24 LIB	25 SAG	24 CAP	25 PIS	24 ARI
25 VIR	26 SCO	27 CAP	26 AQU	27 ARI	26 TAU
28 LIB	29 SAG	29 AQU	28 PIS	29 TAU	29 GEM
30 SCO	31 CAP		31 ARI		31 CAN

1961

JUL	AUG	SEP	OCT	NOV	DEC
1 PIS	2 TAU	1 GEM	3 LEO	2 VIR	1 LIB
4 ARI	4 GEM	3 CAN	5 VIR	4 LIB	4 SCO
6 TAU	7 CAN	5 LEO	8 LIB	6 SCO	6 SAG
8 GEM	9 LEO	8 VIR	10 SCO	9 SAG	8 CAP
10 CAN	12 VIR	10 LIB	13 SAG	11 CAP	10 AQU
13 LEO	14 LIB	13 SCO	15 CAP	13 AQU	13 PIS
15 VIR	17 SCO	15 SAG	17 AQU	15 PIS	15 ARI
18 LIB	19 SAG	18 CAP	19 PIS	17 ARI	17 TAU
20 SCO	21 CAP	20 AQU	21 ARI	20 TAU	19 GEM
23 SAG	23 AQU	22 PIS	23 TAU	22 GEM	21 CAN
25 CAP	25 PIS	24 ARI	25 GEM	24 CAN	24 LEO
27 AQU	27 ARI	26 TAU	28 CAN	26 LEO	26 VIR
29 PIS	29 TAU	28 GEM	30 LEO	29 VIR	29 LIB
31 ARI		30 CAN			31 SCO

1962

JAN	FEB	MAR	APR	MAY	JUN
3 SAG	1 CAP	1 CAP	1 PIS	1 ARI	1 GEM
5 CAP	3 AQU	3 AQU	3 ARI	3 TAU	3 CAN
7 AQU	5 PIS	5 PIS	5 TAU	5 GEM	6 LEO
9 PIS	7 ARI	7 ARI	7 GEM	7 CAN	8 VIR
11 ARI	9 TAU	9 TAU	9 CAN	9 LEO	10 LIB
13 TAU	12 GEM	11 GEM	12 LEO	12 VIR	13 SCO
15 GEM	14 CAN	13 CAN	14 VIR	14 LIB	15 SAG
18 CAN	16 LEO	16 LEO	17 LIB	17 SCO	18 CAP
20 LEO	19 VIR	18 VIR	19 SCO	19 SAG	20 AQU
23 VIR	21 LIB	21 LIB	22 SAG	21 CAP	22 PIS
25 LIB	24 SCO	23 SCO	24 CAP	24 AQU	24 ARI
28 SCO	26 SAG	26 SAG	26 AQU	26 PIS	26 TAU
30 SAG		28 CAP	28 PIS	28 ARI	28 GEM
		30 AQU		30 TAU	

1963

JAN	FEB	MAR	APR	MAY	JUN
1 ARI	2 GEM	1 GEM	2 LEO	2 VIR	3 SCO
4 TAU	4 CAN	3 CAN	4 VIR	4 LIB	5 SAG
6 GEM	6 LEO	6 LEO	7 LIB	7 SCO	8 CAP
8 CAN	9 VIR	8 VIR	9 SCO	9 SAG	10 AQU
10 LEO	11 LIB	11 LIB	12 SAG	12 CAP	12 PIS
12 VIR	14 SCO	13 SCO	14 CAP	14 AQU	15 ARI
15 LIB	16 SAG	16 SAG	17 AQU	16 PIS	17 TAU
17 SCO	19 CAP	18 CAP	19 PIS	18 ARI	19 GEM
20 SAG	21 AQU	20 AQU	21 ARI	20 TAU	21 CAN
22 CAP	23 PIS	23 PIS	23 TAU	22 GEM	23 LEO
25 AQU	25 ARI	25 ARI	25 GEM	24 CAN	25 VIR
27 PIS	27 TAU	27 TAU	27 CAN	27 LEO	28 LIB
29 AIR		29 GEM	29 LEO	29 VIR	30 SCO
31 TAU		31 CAN		31 LIB	

1962

JUL	AUG	SEP	OCT	NOV	DEC
1 CAN	2 VIR	3 SCO	3 SAG	1 CAP	1 AQU
3 LEO	4 LIB	5 SAG	5 CAP	4 AQU	3 PIS
5 VIR	7 SCO	8 CAP	7 AQU	6 PIS	5 ARI
8 LIB	9 SAG	10 AQU	10 PIS	8 ARI	7 TAU
10 SCO	11 CAP	12 PIS	12 ARI	10 TAU	9 GEM
13 SAG	14 AQU	14 ARI	14 TAU	12 GEM	11 CAN
15 CAP	16 PIS	16 TAU	16 GEM	14 CAN	14 LEO
17 AQU	18 ARI	18 GEM	18 CAN	16 LEO	16 VIR
19 PIS	20 TAU	20 CAN	20 LEO	19 VIR	19 LIB
21 ARI	22 GEM	23 LEO	22 VIR	21 LIB	21 SCO
23 TAU	24 CAN	25 VIR	25 LIB	24 SCO	24 SAG
26 GEM	26 LEO	28 LIB	27 SCO	26 SAG	26 CAP
28 CAN	29 VIR	30 SCO	30 SAG	29 CAP	28 AQU
30 LEO	31 LIB				30 PIS

1963

JUL	AUG	SEP	OCT	NOV	DEC
3 SAG	1 CAP	2 PIS	2 ARI	2 GEM	2 CAN
5 CAP	4 AQU	4 ARI	4 TAU	4 CAN	4 LEO
7 AQU	6 PIS	7 TAU	6 GEM	6 LEO	6 VIR
10 PIS	8 ARI	9 GEM	8 CAN	9 VIR	8 LIB
12 ARI	10 TAU	11 CAN	10 LEO	11 LIB	11 SCO
14 TAU	12 GEM	13 LEO	12 VIR	14 SCO	13 SAG
16 GEM	14 CAN	15 VIR	15 LIB	16 SAG	16 CAP
18 CAN	17 LEO	18 LIB	17 SCO	19 CAP	18 AQU
20 LEO	19 VIR	20 SCO	20 SAG	21 AQU	21 PIS
23 VIR	21 LIB	23 SAG	22 CAP	24 PIS	23 ARI
25 LIB	24 SCO	25 CAP	25 AQU	26 ARI	25 TAU
27 SCO	26 SAG	28 AQU	27 PIS	28 TAU	27 GEM
30 SAG	29 CAP	30 PIS	29 ARI	30 GEM	29 CAN
	31 AQU		31 TAU		31 LEO

1964

JAN	FEB	MAR	APR	MAY	JUN
2 VIR	1 LIB	2 SCO	1 SAG	1 CAP	2 PIS
5 LIB	4 SCO	4 SAG	3 CAP	3 AQU	4 ARI
7 SCO	6 SAG	7 CAP	6 AQU	5 PIS	6 TAU
10 SAG	9 CAP	9 AQU	8 PIS	8 ARI	8 GEM
12 CAP	11 AQU	12 PIS	10 ARI	10 TAU	10 CAN
15 AQU	13 PIS	14 ARI	12 TAU	12 GEM	12 LEO
17 PIS	16 ARI	16 TAU	14 GEM	14 CAN	14 VIR
19 ARI	18 TAU	18 GEM	16 CAN	16 LEO	17 LIB
21 TAU	20 GEM	20 CAN	19 LEO	18 VIR	19 SCO
24 GEM	22 CAN	22 LEO	21 VIR	20 LIB	22 SAG
26 CAN	24 LEO	25 VIR	23 LIB	23 SCO	24 CAP
28 LEO	26 VIR	27 LIB	26 SCO	25 SAG	27 AQU
30 VIR	28 LIB	29 SCO	28 SAG	28 CAP	29 PIS
				30 AQU	

1965

JAN	FEB	MAR	APR	MAY	JUN
1 CAP	2 PIS	2 PIS	3 TAU	2 GEM	1 CAN
4 AQU	5 ARI	4 ARI	5 GEM	4 CAN	3 LEO
6 PIS	7 TAU	6 TAU	7 CAN	6 LEO	5 VIR
9 ARI	9 GEM	9 GEM	9 LEO	8 VIR	7 LIB
11 TAU	11 CAN	11 CAN	11 VIR	11 LIB	9 SCO
13 GEM	13 LEO	13 LEO	13 LIB	13 SCO	12 SAG
15 CAN	16 VIR	15 VIR	16 SCO	15 SAG	14 CAP
17 LEO	18 LIB	17 LIB	18 SAG	18 CAP	16 AQU
19 VIR	20 SCO	19 SCO	20 CAP	20 AQU	19 PIS
21 LIB	22 SAG	22 SAG	23 AQU	23 PIS	21 ARI
23 SCO	25 CAP	24 CAP	25 PIS	25 ARI	24 TAU
26 SAG	27 AQU	27 AQU	28 ARI	27 TAU	26 GEM
28 CAP		29 PIS	30 TAU	30 GEM	28 CAN
31 AQU		31 ARI			30 LEO

1964

JUL	AUG	SEP	OCT	NOV	DEC
1 ARI	2 GEM	2 LEO	2 VIR	3 SCO	2 SAG
4 TAU	4 CAN	5 VIR	4 LIB	5 SAG	5 CAP
6 GEM	6 LEO	7 LIB	6 SCO	8 CAP	7 AQU
8 CAN	8 VIR	9 SCO	9 SAG	10 AQU	10 PIS
10 LEO	10 LIB	11 SAG	11 CAP	13 PIS	12 ARI
12 VIR	13 SCO	14 CAP	14 AQU	15 ARI	15 TAU
14 LIB	15 SAG	16 AQU	16 PIS	17 TAU	17 GEM
16 SCO	18 CAP	19 PIS	19 ARI	19 GEM	19 CAN
19 SAG	20 AQU	21 ARI	21 TAU	21 CAN	21 LEO
21 CAP	23 PIS	23 TAU	23 GEM	23 LEO	23 VIR
24 AQU	25 ARI	25 GEM	25 CAN	25 VIR	25 LIB
26 PIS	27 TAU	28 CAN	27 LEO	28 LIB	27 SCO
29 ARI	29 GEM	30 LEO	29 VIR	30 SCO	30 SAG
31 TAU	31 CAN		31 LIB		

1965

JUL	AUG	SEP	OCT	NOV	DEC
2 VIR	3 SCO	1 SAG	1 CAP	2 PIS	2 ARI
4 LIB	5 SAG	4 CAP	4 AQU	5 ARI	5 TAU
6 SCO	7 CAP	6 AQU	6 PIS	7 TAU	7 GEM
9 SAG	10 AQU	9 PIS	9 ARI	9 GEM	9 CAN
11 CAP	13 PIS	11 ARI	11 TAU	12 CAN	11 LEO
14 AQU	15 ARI	14 TAU	13 GEM	14 LEO	13 VIR
16 PIS	17 TAU	16 GEM	15 CAN	16 VIR	15 LIB
19 ARI	20 GEM	18 CAN	17 LEO	18 LIB	17 SCO
21 TAU	22 CAN	20 LEO	20 VIR	20 SCO	20 SAG
23 GEM	24 LEO	22 VIR	22 LIB	22 SAG	22 CAP
25 CAN	26 VIR	24 LIB	24 SCO	25 CAP	25 AQU
27 LEO	28 LIB	26 SCO	26 SAG	27 AQU	27 PIS
29 VIR	30 SCO	29 SAG	28 CAP	30 PIS	30 ARI
31 LIB			31 AQU		

1966

JAN	FEB	MAR	APR	MAY	JUN
1 TAU	2 CAN	1 CAN	2 VIR	1 LIB	2 SAG
3 GEM	4 LEO	3 LEO	4 LIB	3 SCO	4 CAP
5 CAN	6 VIR	5 VIR	6 SCO	5 SAG	6 AQU
7 LEO	8 LIB	7 LIB	8 SAG	8 CAP	9 PIS
9 VIR	10 SCO	9 SCO	10 CAP	10 AQU	11 ARI
11 LIB	12 SAG	12 SAG	13 AQU	12 PIS	14 TAU
14 SCO	15 CAP	14 CAP	15 PIS	15 ARI	16 GEM
16 SAG	17 AQU	16 AQU	18 ARI	17 TAU	18 CAN
18 CAP	20 PIS	19 PIS	20 TAU	20 GEM	20 LEO
21 AQU	22 ARI	21 ARI	22 GEM	22 CAN	23 VIR
23 PIS	25 TAU	24 TAU	25 CAN	24 LEO	25 LIB
26 ARI	27 GEM	26 GEM	27 LEO	26 VIR	27 SCO
28 TAU		29 CAN	29 VIR	28 LIB	29 SAG
31 GEM		31 LEO		31 SCO	

1967

JAN	FEB	MAR	APR	MAY	JUN
2 LIB	3 SAG	2 SAG	3 AQU	2 PIS	1 ARI
4 SCO	5 CAP	4 CAP	5 PIS	5 ARI	4 TAU
6 SAG	7 AQU	6 AQU	8 ARI	7 TAU	6 GEM
9 CAP	10 PIS	9 PIS	10 TAU	10 GEM	9 CAN
11 AQU	12 ARI	11 ARI	13 GEM	12 CAN	11 LEO
13 PIS	15 TAU	14 TAU	15 CAN	15 LEO	13 VIR
16 ARI	17 GEM	16 GEM	17 LEO	17 VIR	15 LIB
18 TAU	19 CAN	19 CAN	20 VIR	19 LIB	17 SCO
21 GEM	22 LEO	21 LEO	22 LIB	21 SCO	19 SAG
23 CAN	24 VIR	23 VIR	24 SCO	23 SAG	21 CAP
25 LEO	26 LIB	25 LIB	26 SAG	25 CAP	24 AQU
27 VIR	28 SCO	27 SCO	28 CAP	27 AQU	26 PIS
29 LIB		29 SAG	30 AQU	30 PIS	28 ARI
31 SCO		31 CAP			

1966

JUL	AUG	SEP	OCT	NOV	DEC
1 CAP	2 PIS	1 ARI	1 TAU	2 CAN	2 LEO
4 AQU	5 ARI	4 TAU	3 GEM	4 LEO	4 VIR
6 PIS	7 TAU	6 GEM	6 CAN	6 VIR	6 LIB
9 ARI	10 GEM	9 CAN	8 LEO	8 LIB	8 SCO
11 TAU	12 CAN	11 LEO	10 VIR	11 SCO	10 SAG
14 GEM	14 LEO	13 VIR	12 LIB	13 SAG	12 CAP
16 CAN	16 VIR	15 LIB	14 SCO	15 CAP	14 AQU
18 LEO	18 LIB	17 SCO	16 SAG	17 AQU	17 PIS
20 VIR	20 SCO	19 SAG	18 CAP	20 PIS	19 ARI
22 LIB	22 SAG	21 CAP	21 AQU	22 ARI	22 TAU
24 SCO	25 CAP	23 AQU	23 PIS	25 TAU	24 GEM
26 SAG	27 AQU	26 PIS	26 ARI	27 GEM	27 CAN
29 CAP	30 PIS	28 ARI	28 TAU	29 CAN	29 LEO
31 AQU			31 GEM		31 VIR

1967

JUL	AUG	SEP	OCT	NOV	DEC
1 TAU	2 CAN	1 LEO	2 LIB	1 SCO	2 CAP
3 GEM	4 LEO	3 VIR	4 SCO	3 SAG	4 AQU
6 CAN	7 VIR	5 LIB	6 SAG	5 CAP	7 PIS
8 LEO	9 LIB	7 SCO	9 CAP	7 AQU	9 ARI
10 VIR	11 SCO	9 SAG	11 AQU	9 PIS	12 TAU
12 LIB	13 SAG	11 CAP	13 PIS	12 ARI	14 GEM
15 SCO	15 CAP	14 AQU	16 ARI	14 TAU	17 CAN
17 SAG	17 AQU	16 PIS	18 TAU	17 GEM	19 LEO
19 CAP	20 PIS	18 ARI	21 GEM	19 CAN	21 VIR
21 AQU	22 ARI	21 TAU	23 CAN	22 LEO	24 LIB
23 PIS	25 TAU	23 GEM	26 LEO	24 VIR	26 SCO
26 ARI	27 GEM	26 CAN	28 VIR	26 LIB	28 SAG
28 TAU	30 CAN	28 LEO	30 LIB	28 SCO	30 CAP
31 GEM		30 VIR		30 SAG	

1968

JAN	FEB	MAR	APR	MAY	JUN
1 AQU	2 ARI	3 TAU	2 GEM	1 CAN	2 VIR
3 PIS	4 TAU	5 GEM	4 CAN	4 LEO	5 LIB
6 ARI	7 GEM	8 CAN	7 LEO	6 VIR	7 SCO
8 TAU	9 CAN	10 LEO	9 VIR	8 LIB	9 SAG
11 GEM	12 LEO	12 VIR	11 LIB	10 SCO	11 CAP
13 CAN	14 VIR	14 LIB	13 SCO	12 SAG	13 AQU
15 LEO	16 LIB	17 SCO	15 SAG	14 CAP	15 PIS
18 VIR	18 SCO	19 SAG	17 CAP	16 AQU	17 ARI
20 LIB	20 SAG	21 CAP	19 AQU	19 PIS	20 TAU
22 SCO	22 CAP	23 AQU	21 PIS	21 ARI	22 GEM
24 SAG	25 AQU	25 PIS	24 ARI	24 TAU	25 CAN
26 CAP	27 PIS	28 ARI	26 TAU	26 GEM	27 LEO
28 AQU	29 ARI	30 TAU	29 GEM	29 CAN	30 VIR
31 PIS				31 LEO	

1969

JAN	FEB	MAR	APR	MAY	JUN
2 CAN	1 LEO	2 VIR	1 LIB	1 SCO	1 CAP
4 LEO	3 VIR	5 LIB	3 SCO	3 SAG	3 AQU
7 VIR	6 LIB	7 SCO	5 SAG	5 CAP	5 PIS
9 LIB	8 SCO	9 SAG	8 CAP	7 AQU	7 ARI
12 SCO	10 SAG	11 CAP	10 AQU	9 PIS	10 TAU
14 SAG	12 CAP	13 AQU	12 PIS	11 ARI	12 GEM
16 CAP	14 AQU	16 PIS	14 ARI	14 TAU	15 CAN
18 AQU	16 PIS	18 ARI	16 TAU	16 GEM	17 LEO
20 PIS	18 ARI	20 TAU	19 GEM	19 CAN	20 VIR
22 ARI	21 TAU	22 GEM	21 CAN	21 LEO	22 LIB
24 TAU	23 GEM	25 CAN	24 LEO	24 VIR	25 SCO
27 GEM	26 CAN	27 LEO	26 VIR	26 LIB	27 SAG
29 CAN	28 LEO	30 VIR	29 LIB	28 SCO	29 CAP
				30 SAG	

1968

JUL	AUG	SEP	OCT	NOV	DEC
2 LIB	3 SAG	1 CAP	2 PIS	1 ARI	1 TAU
4 SCO	5 CAP	3 AQU	5 ARI	3 TAU	3 GEM
6 SAG	7 AQU	5 PIS	7 TAU	6 GEM	6 CAN
8 CAP	9 PIS	7 ARI	10 GEM	8 CAN	8 LEO
10 AQU	11 ARI	10 TAU	12 CAN	11 LEO	11 VIR
12 PIS	13 TAU	12 GEM	15 LEO	13 VIR	13 LIB
15 ARI	16 GEM	15 CAN	17 VIR	16 LIB	15 SCO
17 TAU	18 CAN	17 LEO	19 LIB	18 SCO	17 SAG
20 GEM	21 LEO	20 VIR	21 SCO	20 SAG	19 CAP
22 CAN	23 VIR	22 LIB	23 SAG	22 CAP	21 AQU
25 LEO	25 LIB	24 SCO	25 CAP	24 AQU	23 PIS
27 VIR	28 SCO	26 SAG	27 AQU	26 PIS	26 ARI
29 LIB	30 SAG	28 CAP	30 PIS	28 ARI	28 TAU
31 SCO		30 AQU			30 GEM

1969

JUL	AUG	SEP	OCT	NOV	DEC
1 AQU	1 ARI	2 GEM	2 CAN	1 LEO	1 VIR
3 PIS	3 TAU	5 CAN	4 LEO	3 VIR	3 LIB
5 ARI	6 GEM	7 LEO	7 VIR	6 LIB	5 SCO
7 TAU	8 CAN	10 VIR	9 LIB	8 SCO	8 SAG
10 GEM	11 LEO	12 LIB	12 SCO	10 SAG	10 CAP
12 CAN	13 VIR	14 SCO	14 SAG	12 CAP	12 AQU
15 LEO	16 LIB	17 SAG	16 CAP	14 AQU	14 PIS
17 VIR	18 SCO	19 CAP	18 AQU	16 PIS	16 ARI
20 LIB	20 SAG	21 AQU	20 PIS	19 ARI	18 TAU
22 SCO	22 CAP	23 PIS	22 ARI	21 TAU	20 GEM
24 SAG	24 AQU	25 ARI	25 TAU	23 GEM	23 CAN
26 CAP	26 PIS	27 TAU	27 GEM	26 CAN	25 LEO
28 AQU	29 ARI	29 GEM	29 CAN	28 LEO	28 VIR
30 PIS	31 TAU				30 LIB

1970

JAN	FEB	MAR	APR	MAY	JUN
2 SCO	2 CAP	2 CAP	2 PIS	2 ARI	2 GEM
4 SAG	4 AQU	4 AQU	4 ARI	4 TAU	5 CAN
6 CAP	6 PIS	6 PIS	6 TAU	6 GEM	7 LEO
8 AQU	8 ARI	8 ARI	9 GEM	8 CAN	10 VIR
10 PIS	11 TAU	10 TAU	11 CAN	11 LEO	12 LIB
12 ARI	13 GEM	12 GEM	14 LEO	13 VIR	15 SCO
14 TAU	15 CAN	15 CAN	16 VIR	16 LIB	17 SAG
17 GEM	18 LEO	17 LEO	19 LIB	18 SCO	19 CAP
19 CAN	20 VIR	20 VIR	21 SCO	20 SAG	21 AQU
22 LEO	23 LIB	22 LIB	23 SAG	23 CAP	23 PIS
24 VIR	25 SCO	25 SCO	25 CAP	25 AQU	25 ARI
27 LIB	28 SAG	27 SAG	27 AQU	27 PIS	27 TAU
29 SCO		29 CAP	30 PIS	29 ARI	30 GEM
31 SAG		31 AQU		31 TAU	

1971

JAN	FEB	MAR	APR	MAY	JUN
3 ARI	1 TAU	2 GEM	1 CAN	1 LEO	2 LIB
5 TAU	3 GEM	5 CAN	3 LEO	3 VIR	5 SCO
7 GEM	5 CAN	7 LEO	6 VIR	6 LIB	7 SAG
9 CAN	8 LEO	10 VIR	8 LIB	8 SCO	9 CAP
12 LEO	10 VIR	12 LIB	11 SCO	11 SAG	11 AQU
14 VIR	13 LIB	15 SCO	13 SAG	13 CAP	14 PIS
17 LIB	15 SCO	17 SAG	16 CAP	15 AQU	16 ARI
19 SCO	18 SAG	19 CAP	18 AQU	17 PIS	18 TAU
22 SAG	20 CAP	22 AQU	20 PIS	20 ARI	20 GEM
24 CAP	22 AQU	24 PIS	22 ARI	22 TAU	22 CAN
26 AQU	24 PIS	26 ARI	24 TAU	24 GEM	24 LEO
28 PIS	26 ARI	28 TAU	26 GEM	26 CAN	27 VIR
30 ARI	28 TAU	30 GEM	28 CAN	28 LEO	29 LIB
				30 VIR	

1970

JUL	AUG	SEP	OCT	NOV	DEC
2 CAN	1 LEO	2 LIB	2 SCO	3 CAP	2 AQU
4 LEO	3 VIR	5 SCO	4 SAG	5 AQU	4 PIS
7 VIR	6 LIB	7 SAG	6 CAP	7 PIS	6 ARI
10 LIB	8 SCO	9 CAP	9 AQU	9 ARI	8 TAU
12 SCO	11 SAG	11 AQU	11 PIS	11 TAU	11 GEM
14 SAG	13 CAP	13 PIS	13 ARI	13 GEM	13 CAN
16 CAP	15 AQU	15 ARI	15 TAU	16 CAN	15 LEO
18 AQU	17 PIS	17 TAU	17 GEM	18 LEO	18 VIR
20 PIS	19 ARI	19 GEM	19 CAN	20 VIR	20 LIB
22 ARI	21 TAU	22 CAN	22 LEO	23 LIB	23 SCO
25 TAU	23 GEM	24 LEO	24 VIR	25 SCO	25 SAG
27 GEM	26 CAN	27 VIR	27 LIB	28 SAG	27 CAP
29 CAN	28 LEO	29 LIB	29 SCO	30 CAP	29 AQU
	31 VIR		31 SAG		31 PIS

1971

JUL	AUG	SEP	OCT	NOV	DEC
2 SCO	1 SAG	2 AQU	1 PIS	2 TAU	1 GEM
4 SAG	3 CAP	4 PIS	3 ARI	4 GEM	3 CAN
7 CAP	5 AQU	6 ARI	5 TAU	6 CAN	5 LEO
9 AQU	7 PIS	8 TAU	7 GEM	8 LEO	8 VIR
11 PIS	9 ARI	10 GEM	9 CAN	10 VIR	10 LIB
13 ARI	11 TAU	12 CAN	12 LEO	13 LIB	13 SCO
15 TAU	13 GEM	14 LEO	14 VIR	15 SCO	15 SAG
17 GEM	16 CAN	17 VIR	16 LIB	18 SAG	17 CAP
19 CAN	18 LEO	19 LIB	19 SCO	20 CAP	20 AQU
22 LEO	20 VIR	22 SCO	22 SAG	23 AQU	22 PIS
24 VIR	23 LIB	24 SAG	24 CAP	25 PIS	24 ARI
27 LIB	26 SCO	27 CAP	26 AQU	27 ARI	26 TAU
29 SCO	28 SAG	29 AQU	29 PIS	29 TAU	28 GEM
	30 CAP		31 ARI		30 CAN

1972

JAN	FEB	MAR	APR	MAY	JUN
2 LEO	3 LIB	1 LIB	2 SAG	2 CAP	1 AQU
4 VIR	5 SCO	4 SCO	5 CAP	5 AQU	3 PIS
6 LIB	8 SAG	6 SAG	7 AQU	7 PIS	5 ARI
9 SCO	10 CAP	9 CAP	10 PIS	9 ARI	7 TAU
11 SAG	12 AQU	11 AQU	12 ARI	11 TAU	9 GEM
14 CAP	15 PIS	13 PIS	14 TAU	13 GEM	11 CAN
16 AQU	17 ARI	15 ARI	16 GEM	15 CAN	14 LEO
18 PIS	19 TAU	17 TAU	18 CAN	17 LEO	16 VIR
20 ARI	21 GEM	19 GEM	20 LEO	19 VIR	18 LIB
23 TAU	23 CAN	21 CAN	22 VIR	22 LIB	21 SCO
25 GEM	25 LEO	24 LEO	25 LIB	24 SCO	23 SAG
27 CAN	28 VIR	26 VIR	27 SCO	27 SAG	26 CAP
29 LEO		28 LIB	30 SAG	29 CAP	28 AQU
31 VIR		31 SCO			30 PIS

1973

JAN	FEB	MAR	APR	MAY	JUN
3 CAP	2 AQU	1 AQU	2 ARI	1 TAU	2 CAN
5 AQU	4 PIS	3 PIS	4 TAU	3 GEM	4 LEO
8 PIS	6 ARI	5 ARI	6 GEM	5 CAN	6 VIR
10 ARI	8 TAU	8 TAU	8 CAN	7 LEO	8 LIB
12 TAU	10 GEM	10 GEM	10 LEO	10 VIR	11 SCO
14 GEM	13 CAN	12 CAN	12 VIR	12 LIB	13 SAG
16 CAN	15 LEO	14 LEO	15 LIB	14 SCO	16 CAP
18 LEO	17 VIR	16 VIR	17 SCO	17 SAG	18 AQU
20 VIR	19 LIB	18 LIB	20 SAG	19 CAP	21 PIS
23 LIB	21 SCO	21 SCO	22 CAP	22 AQU	23 ARI
25 SCO	24 SAG	23 SAG	25 AQU	24 PIS	25 TAU
28 SAG	26 CAP	26 CAP	27 PIS	27 ARI	27 GEM
30 CAP		28 AQU	29 ARI	29 TAU	29 CAN
		31 PIS		31 GEM	

1972

JUL	AUG	SEP	OCT	NOV	DEC
3 ARI	1 TAU	1 CAN	1 LEO	2 LIB	1 SCO
5 TAU	3 GEM	4 LEO	3 VIR	4 SCO	4 SAG
7 GEM	5 CAN	6 VIR	5 LIB	7 SAG	7 CAP
9 CAN	7 LEO	8 LIB	8 SCO	9 CAP	9 AQU
11 LEO	10 VIR	11 SCO	10 SAG	12 AQU	11 PIS
13 VIR	12 LIB	13 SAG	13 CAP	14 PIS	14 ARI
15 LIB	14 SCO	16 CAP	15 AQU	16 ARI	16 TAU
18 SCO	17 SAG	18 AQU	18 PIS	18 TAU	18 GEM
20 SAG	19 CAP	20 PIS	20 ARI	20 GEM	20 CAN
23 CAP	22 AQU	22 ARI	22 TAU	22 CAN	22 LEO
25 AQU	24 PIS	24 TAU	24 GEM	24 LEO	24 VIR
28 PIS	26 ARI	27 GEM	26 CAN	27 VIR	26 LIB
30 ARI	28 TAU	29 CAN	28 LEO	29 LIB	29 SCO
	30 GEM		30 VIR		31 SAG

1973

JUL	AUG	SEP	OCT	NOV	DEC
1 LEO	2 LIB	1 SCO	3 CAP	2 AQU	1 PIS
3 VIR	4 SCO	3 SAG	5 AQU	4 PIS	4 ARI
5 LIB	7 SAG	5 CAP	8 PIS	6 ARI	6 TAU
8 SCO	9 CAP	8 AQU	10 ARI	9 TAU	8 GEM
10 SAG	12 AQU	10 PIS	12 TAU	11 GEM	10 CAN
13 CAP	14 PIS	13 ARI	14 GEM	13 CAN	12 LEO
15 AQU	16 ARI	15 TAU	16 CAN	15 LEO	14 VIR
18 PIS	19 TAU	17 GEM	19 LEO	17 VIR	16 LIB
20 ARI	21 GEM	19 CAN	21 VIR	19 LIB	19 SCO
22 TAU	23 CAN	21 LEO	23 LIB	22 SCO	21 SAG
25 GEM	25 LEO	23 VIR	25 SCO	24 SAG	24 CAP
27 CAN	27 VIR	26 LIB	28 SAG	26 CAP	26 AQU
29 LEO	29 LIB	28 SCO	30 CAP	29 AQU	29 PIS
31 VIR		30 SAG			31 ARI

1974

JAN	FEB	MAR	APR	MAY	JUN
2 TAU	1 GEM	2 CAN	1 LEO	2 LIB	1 SCO
5 GEM	3 CAN	4 LEO	3 VIR	4 SCO	3 SAG
7 CAN	5 LEO	7 VIR	5 LIB	7 SAG	6 CAP
9 LEO	7 VIR	9 LIB	7 SCO	9 CAP	9 AQU
11 VIR	9 LIB	11 SCO	9 SAG	12 AQU	11 PIS
13 LIB	11 SCO	13 SAG	12 CAP	14 PIS	13 ARI
15 SCO	14 SAG	16 CAP	14 AQU	17 ARI	15 TAU
17 SAG	16 CAP	18 AQU	17 PIS	19 TAU	18 GEM
20 CAP	19 AQU	21 PIS	19 ARI	21 GEM	20 CAN
22 AQU	21 PIS	23 ARI	22 TAU	23 CAN	22 LEO
25 PIS	24 ARI	25 TAU	24 GEM	25 LEO	24 VIR
27 ARI	26 TAU	27 GEM	26 CAN	27 VIR	26 LIB
30 TAU	28 GEM	30 CAN	28 LEO	30 LIB	28 SCO
			30 VIR		30 SAG

1975

JAN	FEB	MAR	APR	MAY	JUN
1 VIR	2 SCO	1 SCO	2 CAP	2 AQU	3 ARI
3 LIB	4 SAG	3 SAG	4 AQU	4 PIS	5 TAU
5 SCO	6 CAP	5 CAP	7 PIS	7 ARI	8 GEM
8 SAG	9 AQU	8 AQU	9 ARI	9 TAU	10 CAN
10 CAP	11 PIS	10 PIS	12 TAU	11 GEM	12 LEO
12 AQU	14 ARI	13 ARI	14 GEM	14 CAN	14 VIR
15 PIS	16 TAU	15 TAU	16 CAN	16 LEO	16 LIB
17 ARI	19 GEM	18 GEM	19 LEO	18 VIR	18 SCO
20 TAU	21 CAN	20 CAN	21 VIR	20 LIB	21 SAG
22 GEM	23 LEO	22 LEO	23 LIB	22 SCO	23 CAP
24 CAN	25 VIR	24 VIR	25 SCO	24 SAG	25 AQU
26 LEO	27 LIB	26 LIB	27 SAG	27 CAP	28 PIS
28 VIR		28 SCO	29 CAP	29 AQU	30 ARI
30 LIB		30 SAG		31 PIS	

1974

JUL	AUG	SEP	OCT	NOV	DEC
3 CAP	2 AQU	3 ARI	2 TAU	1 GEM	1 CAN
5 AQU	4 PIS	5 TAU	5 GEM	3 CAN	3 LEO
8 PIS	7 ARI	8 GEM	7 CAN	5 LEO	5 VIR
10 ARI	9 TAU	10 CAN	9 LEO	8 VIR	7 LIB
13 TAU	11 GEM	12 LEO	11 VIR	10 LIB	9 SCO
15 GEM	13 CAN	14 VIR	13 LIB	12 SCO	11 SAG
17 CAN	15 LEO	16 LIB	15 SCO	14 SAG	14 CAP
19 LEO	17 VIR	18 SCO	18 SAG	16 CAP	16 AQU
21 VIR	19 LIB	20 SAG	20 CAP	19 AQU	19 PIS
23 LIB	22 SCO	23 CAP	22 AQU	21 PIS	21 ARI
25 SCO	24 SAG	25 AQU	25 PIS	24 ARI	24 TAU
28 SAG	26 CAP	28 PIS	27 ARI	26 TAU	26 GEM
30 CAP	29 AQU	30 ARI	30 TAU	28 GEM	28 CAN
	31 PIS				30 LEO

1975

JUL	AUG	SEP	OCT	NOV	DEC
3 TAU	1 GEM	2 LEO	2 VIR	2 SCO	2 SAG
5 GEM	4 CAN	4 VIR	4 LIB	4 SAG	4 CAP
7 CAN	6 LEO	6 LIB	6 SCO	6 CAP	6 AQU
9 LEO	8 VIR	8 SCO	8 SAG	9 AQU	8 PIS
11 VIR	10 LIB	10 SAG	10 CAP	11 PIS	11 ARI
14 LIB	12 SCO	13 CAP	12 AQU	14 ARI	13 TAU
16 SCO	14 SAG	15 AQU	15 PIS	16 TAU	16 GEM
18 SAG	16 CAP	18 PIS	17 ARI	19 GEM	18 CAN
20 CAP	19 AQU	20 ARI	20 TAU	21 CAN	20 LEO
23 AQU	21 PIS	23 TAU	22 GEM	23 LEO	23 VIR
25 PIS	24 ARI	25 GEM	25 CAN	25 VIR	25 LIB
28 ARI	26 TAU	27 CAN	27 LEO	27 LIB	27 SCO
30 TAU	29 GEM	30 LEO	29 VIR	30 SCO	29 SAG
	31 CAN		31 LIB		31 CAP

1976

JAN	FEB	MAR	APR	MAY	JUN
2 AQU	1 PIS	2 ARI	1 TAU	3 CAN	1 LEO
5 PIS	4 ARI	4 TAU	3 GEM	5 LEO	4 VIR
7 ARI	6 TAU	7 GEM	6 CAN	7 VIR	6 LIB
10 TAU	9 GEM	9 CAN	8 LEO	10 LIB	8 SCO
12 GEM	11 CAN	12 LEO	10 VIR	12 SCO	10 SAG
15 CAN	13 LEO	14 VIR	12 LIB	14 SAG	12 CAP
17 LEO	15 VIR	16 LIB	14 SCO	16 CAP	14 AQU
19 VIR	17 LIB	18 SCO	16 SAG	18 AQU	17 PIS
21 LIB	19 SCO	20 SAG	18 CAP	20 PIS	19 ARI
23 SCO	21 SAG	22 CAP	20 AQU	23 ARI	22 TAU
25 SAG	24 CAP	24 AQU	23 PIS	25 TAU	24 GEM
27 CAP	26 AQU	27 PIS	25 ARI	28 GEM	26 CAN
30 AQU	28 PIS	29 ARI	28 TAU	30 CAN	29 LEO
			30 GEM		

1977

JAN	FEB	MAR	APR	MAY	JUN
1 GEM	2 LEO	2 LEO	2 LIB	2 SCO	2 CAP
4 CAN	5 VIR	4 VIR	5 SCO	4 SAG	4 AQU
6 LEO	7 LIB	6 LIB	7 SAG	6 CAP	7 PIS
8 VIR	9 SCO	8 SCO	9 CAP	8 AQU	9 ARI
10 LIB	11 SAG	10 SAG	11 AQU	10 PIS	11 TAU
13 SCO	13 CAP	12 CAP	13 PIS	13 ARI	14 GEM
15 SAG	15 AQU	15 AQU	15 ARI	15 TAU	16 CAN
17 CAP	17 PIS	17 PIS	18 TAU	18 GEM	19 LEO
19 AQU	20 ARI	19 ARI	20 GEM	20 CAN	21 VIR
21 PIS	22 TAU	22 TAU	23 CAN	23 LEO	24 LIB
23 ARI	25 GEM	24 GEM	25 LEO	25 VIR	26 SCO
26 TAU	27 CAN	27 CAN	28 VIR	27 LIB	28 SAG
28 GEM		29 LEO	30 LIB	29 SCO	30 CAP
31 CAN		31 VIR		31 SAG	

1976

JUL	AUG	SEP	OCT	NOV	DEC
1 VIR	1 SCO	2 CAP	1 AQU	2 ARI	2 TAU
3 LIB	4 SAG	4 AQU	4 PIS	5 TAU	5 GEM
5 SCO	6 CAP	7 PIS	6 ARI	8 GEM	7 CAN
7 SAG	8 AQU	9 ARI	9 TAU	10 CAN	10 LEO
9 CAP	10 PIS	11 TAU	11 GEM	12 LEO	12 VIR
12 AQU	13 ARI	14 GEM	14 CAN	15 VIR	14 LIB
14 PIS	15 TAU	17 CAN	16 LEO	17 LIB	16 SCO
16 ARI	18 GEM	19 LEO	18 VIR	19 SCO	18 SAG
19 TAU	20 CAN	21 VIR	21 LIB	21 SAG	20 CAP
21 GEM	22 LEO	23 LIB	23 SCO	23 CAP	22 AQU
24 CAN	25 VIR	25 SCO	25 SAG	25 AQU	25 PIS
26 LEO	27 LIB	27 SAG	27 CAP	27 PIS	27 ARI
28 VIR	29 SCO	29 CAP	29 AQU	30 ARI	30 TAU
30 LIB	31 SAG		31 PIS		

1977

JUL	AUG	SEP	OCT	NOV	DEC
2 AQU	3 ARI	1 TAU	1 GEM	3 LEO	2 VIR
4 PIS	5 TAU	4 GEM	4 CAN	5 VIR	5 LIB
6 ARI	7 GEM	6 CAN	6 LEO	7 LIB	7 SCO
9 TAU	10 CAN	9 LEO	9 VIR	9 SCO	9 SAG
11 GEM	12 LEO	11 VIR	11 LIB	11 SAG	11 CAP
14 CAN	15 VIR	13 LIB	13 SCO	13 CAP	13 AQU
16 LEO	17 LIB	16 SCO	15 SAG	15 AQU	15 PIS
19 VIR	19 SCO	18 SAG	17 CAP	18 PIS	17 ARI
21 LIB	21 SAG	20 CAP	19 AQU	20 ARI	19 TAU
23 SCO	24 CAP	22 AQU	21 PIS	22 TAU	22 GEM
25 SAG	26 AQU	24 PIS	24 ARI	25 GEM	25 CAN
27 CAP	28 PIS	26 ARI	26 TAU	27 CAN	27 LEO
29 AQU	30 ARI	29 TAU	28 GEM	30 LEO	30 VIR
31 PIS			31 CAN		

1978

JAN	FEB	MAR	APR	MAY	JUN
1 LIB	2 SAG	1 SAG	1 AQU	1 PIS	1 TAU
3 SCO	4 CAP	3 CAP	3 PIS	3 ARI	4 GEM
5 SAG	6 AQU	5 AQU	6 ARI	5 TAU	6 CAN
7 CAP	8 PIS	7 PIS	8 TAU	8 GEM	9 LEO
9 AQU	10 ARI	9 ARI	10 GEM	10 CAN	11 VIR
11 PIS	12 TAU	12 TAU	13 CAN	13 LEO	14 LIB
13 ARI	15 GEM	14 GEM	15 LEO	15 VIR	16 SCO
16 TAU	17 CAN	16 CAN	18 VIR	17 LIB	18 SAG
18 GEM	20 LEO	19 LEO	20 LIB	20 SCO	20 CAP
21 CAN	22 VIR	21 VIR	22 SCO	22 SAG	22 AQU
23 LEO	24 LIB	24 LIB	24 SAG	24 CAP	24 PIS
26 VIR	27 SCO	26 SCO	26 CAP	26 AQU	26 ARI
28 LIB		28 SAG	29 AQU	28 PIS	29 TAU
30 SCO		30 CAP		30 ARI	

1979

JAN	FEB	MAR	APR	MAY	JUN
2 PIS	2 TAU	2 TAU	3 CAN	2 LEO	1 VIR
4 ARI	5 GEM	4 GEM	5 LEO	5 VIR	4 LIB
6 TAU	7 CAN	6 CAN	8 VIR	7 LIB	6 SCO
8 GEM	9 LEO	9 LEO	10 LIB	10 SCO	8 SAG
11 CAN	12 VIR	11 VIR	12 SCO	12 SAG	11 CAP
13 LEO	15 LIB	14 LIB	15 SAG	14 CAP	13 AQU
16 VIR	17 SCO	16 SCO	17 CAP	16 AQU	15 PIS
18 LIB	19 SAG	19 SAG	19 AQU	18 PIS	17 ARI
21 SCO	21 CAP	21 CAP	21 PIS	21 ARI	19 TAU
23 SAG	24 AQU	23 AQU	23 ARI	23 TAU	21 GEM
25 CAP	26 PIS	25 PIS	25 TAU	25 GEM	24 CAN
27 AQU	28 ARI	27 ARI	28 GEM	27 CAN	26 LEO
29 PIS		29 TAU	30 CAN	30 LEO	29 VIR
31 ARI		31 GEM			

1978

JUL	AUG	SEP	OCT	NOV	DEC
1 GEM	2 LEO	1 VIR	1 LIB	2 SAG	1 CAP
4 CAN	5 VIR	4 LIB	3 SCO	4 CAP	3 AQU
6 LEO	7 LIB	6 SCO	5 SAG	6 AQU	5 PIS
9 VIR	10 SCO	8 SAG	8 CAP	8 PIS	7 ARI
11 LIB	12 SAG	10 CAP	10 AQU	10 ARI	10 TAU
13 SCO	14 CAP	12 AQU	12 PIS	12 TAU	12 GEM
16 SAG	16 AQU	14 PIS	14 ARI	15 GEM	14 CAN
18 CAP	18 PIS	17 ARI	16 TAU	17 CAN	17 LEO
20 AQU	20 ARI	19 TAU	18 GEM	20 LEO	19 VIR
22 PIS	22 TAU	21 GEM	21 CAN	22 VIR	22 LIB
24 ARI	25 GEM	23 CAN	23 LEO	25 LIB	24 SCO
26 TAU	27 CAN	26 LEO	26 VIR	27 SCO	27 SAG
28 GEM	30 LEO	28 VIR	28 LIB	29 SAG	29 CAP
31 CAN			31 SCO		31 AQU

1979

JUL	AUG	SEP	OCT	NOV	DEC
1 LIB	2 SAG	1 CAP	2 PIS	1 ARI	2 GEM
4 SCO	4 CAP	3 AQU	4 ARI	3 TAU	4 CAN
6 SAG	6 AQU	5 PIS	6 TAU	5 GEM	7 LEO
8 CAP	8 PIS	7 ARI	8 GEM	7 CAN	9 VIR
10 AQU	10 ARI	9 TAU	11 CAN	9 LEO	12 LIB
12 PIS	13 TAU	11 GEM	13 LEO	12 VIR	14 SCO
14 ARI	15 GEM	13 CAN	16 VIR	14 LIB	17 SAG
16 TAU	17 CAN	16 LEO	18 LIB	17 SCO	19 CAP
19 GEM	20 LEO	18 VIR	21 SCO	19 SAG	21 AQU
21 CAN	22 VIR	21 LIB	23 SAG	22 CAP	23 PIS
23 LEO	25 LIB	23 SCO	25 CAP	24 AQU	25 ARI
26 VIR	27 SCO	26 SAG	28 AQU	26 PIS	27 TAU
28 LIB	30 SAG	28 CAP	30 PIS	28 ARI	30 GEM
31 SCO		30 AQU		30 TAU	

1980

JAN	FEB	MAR	APR	MAY	JUN
1 CAN	2 VIR	3 LIB	2 SCO	1 SAG	2 AQU
3 LEO	4 LIB	5 SCO	4 SAG	4 CAP	4 PIS
6 VIR	7 SCO	8 SAG	6 CAP	6 AQU	6 ARI
8 LIB	9 SAG	10 CAP	9 AQU	8 PIS	9 TAU
11 SCO	12 CAP	12 AQU	11 PIS	10 ARI	11 GEM
13 SAG	14 AQU	14 PIS	13 ARI	12 TAU	13 CAN
15 CAP	16 PIS	16 ARI	15 TAU	14 GEM	15 LEO
17 AQU	18 ARI	18 TAU	17 GEM	16 CAN	17 VIR
19 PIS	20 TAU	20 GEM	19 CAN	19 LEO	20 LIB
21 ARI	22 GEM	23 CAN	21 LEO	21 VIR	22 SCO
24 TAU	24 CAN	25 LEO	24 VIR	24 LIB	25 SAG
26 GEM	27 LEO	27 VIR	26 LIB	26 SCO	27 CAP
28 CAN	29 VIR	30 LIB	29 SCO	29 SAG	29 AQU
30 LEO				31 CAP	

1981

JAN	FEB	MAR	APR	MAY	JUN
2 SAG	1 CAP	2 AQU	1 PIS	1 ARI	1 GEM
4 CAP	3 AQU	5 PIS	3 ARI	3 TAU	3 CAN
7 AQU	5 PIS	7 ARI	5 TAU	5 GEM	5 LEO
9 PIS	7 ARI	9 TAU	7 GEM	7 CAN	7 VIR
11 ARI	9 TAU	11 GEM	9 CAN	9 LEO	10 LIB
13 TAU	12 GEM	13 CAN	11 LEO	11 VIR	12 SCO
15 GEM	14 CAN	15 LEO	14 VIR	13 LIB	15 SAG
17 CAN	16 LEO	18 VIR	16 LIB	16 SCO	17 CAP
20 LEO	18 VIR	20 LIB	19 SCO	18 SAG	20 AQU
22 VIR	21 LIB	22 SCO	21 SAG	21 CAP	22 PIS
24 LIB	23 SCO	25 SAG	24 CAP	23 AQU	24 ARI
27 SCO	26 SAG	27 CAP	26 AQU	26 PIS	26 TAU
29 SAG	28 CAP	30 AQU	28 PIS	28 ARI	28 GEM
				30 TAU	30 CAN

1980

JUL	AUG	SEP	OCT	NOV	DEC
2 PIS	2 TAU	3 CAN	2 LEO	1 VIR	1 LIB
4 ARI	4 GEM	5 LEO	5 VIR	3 LIB	3 SCO
6 TAU	6 CAN	7 VIR	7 LIB	6 SCO	6 SAG
8 GEM	9 LEO	10 LIB	10 SCO	8 SAG	8 CAP
10 CAN	11 VIR	12 SCO	12 SAG	11 CAP	10 AQU
12 LEO	14 LIB	15 SAG	15 CAP	13 AQU	13 PIS
15 VIR	16 SCO	17 CAP	17 AQU	15 PIS	15 ARI
17 LIB	19 SAG	20 AQU	19 PIS	18 ARI	17 TAU
20 SCO	21 CAP	22 PIS	21 ARI	20 TAU	19 GEM
22 SAG	23 AQU	24 ARI	23 TAU	22 GEM	21 CAN
25 CAP	25 PIS	26 TAU	25 GEM	24 CAN	23 LEO
27 AQU	27 ARI	28 GEM	27 CAN	26 LEO	25 VIR
29 PIS	29 TAU	30 CAN	29 LEO	28 VIR	28 LIB
31 ARI	31 GEM				30 SCO

1981

JUL	AUG	SEP	OCT	NOV	DEC
2 LEO	1 VIR	2 SCO	2 SAG	1 CAP	1 AQU
5 VIR	3 LIB	5 SAG	5 CAP	3 AQU	3 PIS
7 LIB	6 SCO	7 CAP	7 AQU	6 PIS	5 ARI
10 SCO	8 SAG	10 AQU	9 PIS	8 ARI	7 TAU
12 SAG	11 CAP	12 PIS	11 ARI	10 TAU	9 GEM
15 CAP	13 AQU	14 ARI	13 TAU	12 GEM	11 CAN
17 AQU	16 PIS	16 TAU	15 GEM	14 CAN	13 LEO
19 PIS	18 ARI	18 GEM	18 CAN	16 LEO	16 VIR
21 ARI	20 TAU	20 CAN	20 LEO	18 VIR	18 LIB
24 TAU	22 GEM	22 LEO	22 VIR	21 LIB	20 SCO
26 GEM	24 CAN	25 VIR	24 LIB	23 SCO	23 SAG
28 CAN	26 LEO	27 LIB	27 SCO	26 SAG	25 CAP
30 LEO	28 VIR	29 SCO	29 SAG	28 CAP	28 AQU
	31 LIB				30 PIS

1982

JAN	FEB	MAR	APR	MAY	JUN
2 ARI	2 GEM	1 GEM	2 LEO	1 VIR	2 SCO
4 TAU	4 CAN	3 CAN	4 VIR	4 LIB	5 SAG
6 GEM	6 LEO	6 LEO	6 LIB	6 SCO	7 CAP
8 CAN	8 VIR	8 VIR	9 SCO	8 SAG	10 AQU
10 LEO	11 LIB	10 LIB	11 SAG	11 CAP	12 PIS
12 VIR	13 SCO	12 SCO	14 CAP	13 AQU	15 ARI
14 LIB	15 SAG	15 SAG	16 AQU	16 PIS	17 TAU
17 SCO	18 CAP	17 CAP	19 PIS	18 ARI	19 GEM
19 SAG	20 AQU	20 AQU	21 ARI	20 TAU	21 CAN
22 CAP	23 PIS	22 PIS	23 TAU	22 GEM	23 LEO
24 AQU	25 ARI	24 ARI	25 GEM	24 CAN	25 VIR
26 PIS	27 TAU	27 TAU	27 CAN	26 LEO	27 LIB
29 ARI		29 GEM	29 LEO	29 VIR	29 SCO
31 TAU		31 CAN		31 LIB	

1983

JAN	FEB	MAR	APR	MAY	JUN
2 VIR	1 LIB	2 SCO	1 SAG	1 CAP	2 PIS
4 LIB	3 SCO	5 SAG	3 CAP	3 AQU	5 ARI
7 SCO	5 SAG	7 CAP	6 AQU	6 PIS	7 TAU
9 SAG	8 CAP	10 AQU	8 PIS	8 ARI	9 GEM
12 CAP	10 AQU	12 PIS	11 ARI	11 TAU	11 CAN
14 AQU	13 PIS	15 ARI	13 TAU	13 GEM	13 LEO
17 PIS	15 ARI	17 TAU	15 GEM	15 CAN	15 VIR
19 ARI	18 TAU	19 GEM	18 CAN	17 LEO	17 LIB
21 TAU	20 GEM	21 CAN	20 LEO	19 VIR	20 SCO
24 GEM	22 CAN	23 LEO	22 VIR	21 LIB	22 SAG
26 CAN	24 LEO	26 VIR	24 LIB	23 SCO	24 CAP
28 LEO	26 VIR	28 LIB	26 SCO	26 SAG	27 AQU
30 VIR	28 LIB	30 SCO	28 SAG	28 CAP	29 PIS
				31 AQU	

1982

JUL	AUG	SEP	OCT	NOV	DEC
2 SAG	1 CAP	2 PIS	2 ARI	2 GEM	2 CAN
4 CAP	3 AQU	4 ARI	4 TAU	4 CAN	4 LEO
7 AQU	6 PIS	7 TAU	6 GEM	6 LEO	6 VIR
9 PIS	8 ARI	9 GEM	8 CAN	9 VIR	8 LIB
12 ARI	10 TAU	11 CAN	10 LEO	11 LIB	10 SCO
14 TAU	13 GEM	13 LEO	12 VIR	13 SCO	13 SAG
16 GEM	15 CAN	15 VIR	15 LIB	15 SAG	15 CAP
18 CAN	17 LEO	17 LIB	17 SCO	18 CAP	18 AQU
20 LEO	19 VIR	19 SCO	19 SAG	21 AQU	20 PIS
22 VIR	21 LIB	22 SAG	22 CAP	23 PIS	23 ARI
24 LIB	23 SCO	24 CAP	24 AQU	25 ARI	25 TAU
27 SCO	25 SAG	27 AQU	27 PIS	28 TAU	27 GEM
29 SAG	28 CAP	29 PIS	29 ARI	30 GEM	29 CAN
	31 AQU		31 TAU		31 LEO

1983

JUL	AUG	SEP	OCT	NOV	DEC
2 ARI	1 TAU	1 CAN	1 LEO	1 LIB	1 SCO
4 TAU	3 GEM	3 LEO	3 VIR	3 SCO	3 SAG
7 GEM	5 CAN	5 VIR	5 LIB	6 SAG	5 CAP
9 CAN	7 LEO	7 LIB	7 SCO	8 CAP	8 AQU
11 LEO	9 VIR	10 SCO	9 SAG	10 AQU	10 PIS
13 VIR	11 LIB	12 SAG	11 CAP	13 PIS	13 ARI
15 LIB	13 SCO	14 CAP	14 AQU	15 ARI	15 TAU
17 SCO	15 SAG	17 AQU	16 PIS	18 TAU	17 GEM
19 SAG	18 CAP	19 PIS	19 ARI	20 GEM	20 CAN
22 CAP	20 AQU	22 ARI	21 TAU	22 CAN	22 LEO
24 AQU	23 PIS	24 TAU	24 GEM	24 LEO	24 VIR
27 PIS	25 ARI	26 GEM	26 CAN	26 VIR	26 LIB
29 ARI	28 TAU	29 CAN	28 LEO	29 LIB	28 SCO
	30 GEM		30 VIR		30 SAG

1984

JAN	FEB	MAR	APR	MAY	JUN
2 CAP	3 PIS	1 PIS	2 TAU	2 GEM	1 CAN
4 AQU	5 ARI	4 ARI	5 GEM	4 CAN	3 LEO
6 PIS	8 TAU	6 TAU	7 CAN	6 LEO	5 VIR
9 ARI	10 GEM	8 GEM	9 LEO	9 VIR	7 LIB
11 TAU	12 CAN	11 CAN	11 VIR	11 LIB	9 SCO
14 GEM	15 LEO	13 LEO	13 LIB	13 SCO	11 SAG
16 CAN	17 VIR	15 VIR	15 SCO	15 SAG	13 CAP
18 LEO	19 LIB	17 LIB	17 SAG	17 CAP	16 AQU
20 VIR	21 SCO	19 SCO	20 CAP	19 AQU	18 PIS
22 LIB	23 SAG	21 SAG	22 AQU	22 PIS	21 ARI
24 SCO	25 CAP	23 CAP	25 PIS	24 ARI	23 TAU
26 SAG	28 AQU	26 AQU	27 ARI	27 TAU	26 GEM
29 CAP		28 PIS	30 TAU	29 GEM	28 CAN
31 AQU		31 ARI			30 LEO

1985

JAN	FEB	MAR	APR	MAY	JUN
3 GEM	2 CAN	1 CAN	2 VIR	1 LIB	2 SAG
5 CAN	4 LEO	3 LEO	4 LIB	3 SCO	4 CAP
7 LEO	6 VIR	5 VIR	6 SCO	5 SAG	6 AQU
9 VIR	8 LIB	7 LIB	8 SAG	7 CAP	8 PIS
12 LIB	10 SCO	9 SCO	10 CAP	9 AQU	11 ARI
14 SCO	12 SAG	11 SAG	12 AQU	12 PIS	13 TAU
16 SAG	14 CAP	14 CAP	14 PIS	14 ARI	16 GEM
18 CAP	17 AQU	16 AQU	17 ARI	17 TAU	18 CAN
20 AQU	19 PIS	18 PIS	20 TAU	19 GEM	20 LEO
23 PIS	21 ARI	21 ARI	22 GEM	22 CAN	23 VIR
25 ARI	24 TAU	23 TAU	25 CAN	24 LEO	25 LIB
28 TAU	27 GEM	26 GEM	27 LEO	26 VIR	27 SCO
30 GEM		28 CAN	29 VIR	29 LIB	29 SAG
		31 LEO		31 SCO	

1984

JUL	AUG	SEP	OCT	NOV	DEC
2 VIR	3 SCO	1 SAG	1 CAP	2 PIS	1 ARI
4 LIB	5 SAG	3 CAP	3 AQU	4 ARI	4 TAU
6 SCO	7 CAP	6 AQU	5 PIS	7 TAU	6 GEM
9 SAG	9 AQU	8 PIS	8 ARI	9 GEM	9 CAN
11 CAP	12 PIS	11 ARI	10 TAU	12 CAN	11 LEO
13 AQU	14 ARI	13 TAU	13 GEM	14 LEO	13 VIR
16 PIS	17 TAU	16 GEM	15 CAN	16 VIR	15 LIB
18 ARI	19 GEM	18 CAN	18 LEO	18 LIB	17 SCO
21 TAU	22 CAN	20 LEO	20 VIR	20 SCO	20 SAG
23 GEM	24 LEO	22 VIR	22 LIB	22 SAG	22 CAP
25 CAN	26 VIR	24 LIB	24 SCO	24 CAP	24 AQU
27 LEO	28 LIB	26 SCO	26 SAG	27 AQU	26 PIS
29 VIR	30 SCO	28 SAG	28 CAP	29 PIS	29 ARI
31 LIB			30 AQU		31 TAU

1985

JUL	AUG	SEP	OCT	NOV	DEC
1 CAP	2 PIS	1 ARI	3 GEM	2 CAN	1 LEO
3 AQU	4 ARI	3 TAU	5 CAN	4 LEO	4 VIR
5 PIS	7 TAU	6 GEM	8 LEO	6 VIR	6 LIB
8 ARI	9 GEM	8 CAN	10 VIR	9 LIB	8 SCO
10 TAU	12 CAN	10 LEO	12 LIB	11 SCO	10 SAG
13 GEM	14 LEO	13 VIR	14 SCO	13 SAG	12 CAP
15 CAN	16 VIR	15 LIB	16 SAG	15 CAP	14 AQU
18 LEO	18 LIB	17 SCO	18 CAP	17 AQU	16 PIS
20 VIR	20 SCO	19 SAG	20 AQU	19 PIS	19 ARI
22 LIB	22 SAG	21 CAP	23 PIS	21 ARI	21 TAU
24 SCO	25 CAP	23 AQU	25 ARI	24 TAU	24 GEM
26 SAG	27 AQU	25 PIS	28 TAU	26 GEM	26 CAN
28 CAP	29 PIS	28 ARI	20 GEM	29 CAN	29 LEO
31 AQU		30 TAU			31 VIR

1986

JAN	FEB	MAR	APR	MAY	JUN
2 LIB	1 SCO	2 SAG	2 AQU	2 PIS	3 TAU
4 SCO	3 SAG	4 CAP	5 PIS	4 ARI	5 GEM
6 SAG	5 CAP	6 AQU	7 ARI	7 TAU	8 CAN
8 CAP	7 AQU	8 PIS	9 TAU	9 GEM	11 LEO
11 AQU	9 PIS	11 ARI	12 GEM	12 CAN	13 VIR
13 PIS	11 ARI	13 TAU	14 CAN	14 LEO	15 LIB
15 ARI	14 TAU	16 GEM	17 LEO	17 VIR	17 SCO
17 TAU	16 GEM	18 CAN	19 VIR	19 LIB	19 SAG
20 GEM	19 CAN	21 LEO	21 LIB	21 SCO	21 CAP
22 CAN	21 LEO	23 VIR	24 SCO	23 SAG	23 AQU
25 LEO	24 VIR	25 LIB	26 SAG	25 CAP	26 PIS
27 VIR	26 LIB	27 SCO	28 CAP	27 AQU	28 ARI
29 LIB	28 SCO	29 SAG	30 AQU	29 PIS	30 TAU
		31 CAP		31 ARI	

1987

JAN	FEB	MAR	APR	MAY	JUN
1 AQU	1 ARI	1 ARI	2 GEM	2 CAN	3 VIR
3 PIS	4 TAU	3 TAU	4 CAN	4 LEO	5 LIB
5 ARI	6 GEM	5 GEM	7 LEO	7 VIR	8 SCO
7 TAU	9 CAN	8 CAN	9 VIR	9 LIB	10 SAG
10 GEM	11 LEO	10 LEO	12 LIB	11 SCO	12 CAP
12 CAN	14 VIR	13 VIR	14 SCO	13 SAG	14 AQU
15 LEO	16 LIB	15 LIB	16 SAG	15 CAP	16 PIS
17 VIR	18 SCO	18 SCO	18 CAP	17 AQU	18 ARI
20 LIB	21 SAG	20 SAG	20 AQU	20 PIS	20 TAU
22 SCO	23 CAP	22 CAP	22 PIS	22 ARI	23 GEM
24 SAG	25 AQU	24 AQU	25 ARI	24 TAU	25 CAN
26 CAP	27 PIS	26 PIS	27 TAU	26 GEM	28 LEO
28 AQU		28 ARI	29 GEM	29 CAN	30 VIR
30 PIS		30 TAU		31 LEO	

1986

JUL	AUG	SEP	OCT	NOV	DEC
3 GEM	2 CAN	3 VIR	2 LIB	1 SCO	2 CAP
5 CAN	4 LEO	5 LIB	4 SCO	3 SAG	4 AQU
8 LEO	6 VIR	7 SCO	7 SAG	5 CAP	6 PIS
10 VIR	9 LIB	9 SAG	9 CAP	7 AQU	9 ARI
12 LIB	11 SCO	11 CAP	11 AQU	9 PIS	11 TAU
15 SCO	13 SAG	14 AQU	13 PIS	11 ARI	14 GEM
17 SAG	15 CAP	16 PIS	15 ARI	14 TAU	16 CAN
19 CAP	17 AQU	18 ARI	18 TAU	16 GEM	19 LEO
21 AQU	19 PIS	20 TAU	20 GEM	29 CAN	21 VIR
23 PIS	22 ARI	23 GEM	23 CAN	21 LEO	24 LIB
25 ARI	24 TAU	25 CAN	25 LEO	24 VIR	26 SCO
28 TAU	26 GEM	28 LEO	27 VIR	26 LIB	28 SAG
30 GEM	29 CAN	30 VIR	30 LIB	28 SCO	30 CAP
	31 LEO			30 SAG	

1987

JUL	AUG	SEP	OCT	NOV	DEC
3 LIB	1 SCO	2 CAP	1 AQU	2 ARI	1 TAU
5 SCO	4 SAG	4 AQU	3 PIS	4 TAU	4 GEM
7 SAG	6 CAP	6 PIS	6 ARI	6 GEM	6 CAN
9 CAP	8 AQU	8 ARI	8 TAU	9 CAN	8 LEO
11 AQU	10 PIS	10 TAU	10 GEM	11 LEO	11 VIR
13 PIS	12 ARI	13 GEM	12 CAN	14 VIR	14 LIB
15 ARI	14 TAU	15 CAN	15 LEO	16 LIB	16 SCO
18 TAU	16 GEM	17 LEO	17 VIR	18 SCO	18 SAG
20 GEM	19 CAN	20 VIR	20 LIB	21 SAG	20 CAP
22 CAN	21 LEO	22 LIB	22 SCO	23 CAP	22 AQU
25 LEO	24 VIR	25 SCO	24 SAG	25 AQU	24 PIS
27 VIR	26 LIB	27 SAG	26 CAP	27 PIS	26 ARI
30 LIB	29 SCO	29 CAP	29 AQU	29 ARI	29 TAU
	31 SAG		31 PIS		31 GEM

1988

JAN	FEB	MAR	APR	MAY	JUN
2 CAN	1 LEO	2 VIR	1 LIB	3 SAG	1 CAP
5 LEO	4 VIR	4 LIB	3 SCO	5 CAP	3 AQU
7 VIR	6 LIB	7 SCO	5 SAG	7 AQU	5 PIS
10 LIB	9 SCO	9 SAG	8 CAP	9 PIS	8 ARI
12 SCO	11 SAG	11 CAP	10 AQU	11 ARI	10 TAU
15 SAG	13 CAP	14 AQU	12 PIS	13 TAU	12 GEM
17 CAP	15 AQU	16 PIS	14 ARI	16 GEM	14 CAN
19 AQU	17 PIS	18 ARI	16 TAU	18 CAN	17 LEO
21 PIS	19 ARI	20 TAU	18 GEM	20 LEO	19 VIR
23 ARI	21 TAU	22 GEM	20 CAN	23 VIR	22 LIB
25 TAU	23 GEM	24 CAN	23 LEO	25 LIB	24 SCO
27 GEM	26 CAN	27 LEO	25 VIR	28 SCO	26 SAG
30 CAN	28 LEO	29 VIR	28 LIB	30 SAG	29 CAP
			30 SCO		

1989

JAN	FEB	MAR	APR	MAY	JUN
1 SCO	2 CAP	2 CAP	2 PIS	2 ARI	2 GEM
4 SAG	4 AQU	4 AQU	4 ARI	4 TAU	4 CAN
6 CAP	6 PIS	6 PIS	6 TAU	6 GEM	7 LEO
8 AQU	8 ARI	8 ARI	8 GEM	8 CAN	9 VIR
10 PIS	11 TAU	10 TAU	11 CAN	10 LEO	11 LIB
12 ARI	13 GEM	12 GEM	13 LEO	13 VIR	14 SCO
14 TAU	15 CAN	14 CAN	15 VIR	15 LIB	16 SAG
16 GEM	17 LEO	17 LEO	18 LIB	18 SCO	19 CAP
19 CAN	20 VIR	19 VIR	20 SCO	20 SAG	21 AQU
21 LEO	22 LIB	22 LIB	23 SAG	22 CAP	23 PIS
23 VIR	25 SCO	24 SCO	25 CAP	25 AQU	25 ARI
26 LIB	27 SAG	27 SAG	28 AQU	27 PIS	27 TAU
29 SCO		29 CAP	30 PIS	29 ARI	30 GEM
31 SAG		31 AQU		31 TAU	

1988

JUL	AUG	SEP	OCT	NOV	DEC
1 AQU	1 ARI	2 GEM	1 CAN	2 VIR	2 LIB
3 PIS	3 TAU	4 CAN	4 LEO	5 LIB	5 SCO
5 ARI	5 GEM	6 LEO	6 VIR	7 SCO	7 SAG
7 TAU	8 CAN	9 VIR	9 LIB	10 SAG	9 CAP
9 GEM	10 LEO	11 LIB	11 SCO	12 CAP	12 AQU
11 CAN	13 VIR	14 SCO	14 SAG	14 AQU	14 PIS
14 LEO	15 LIB	16 SAG	16 CAP	17 PIS	16 ARI
16 VIR	18 SCO	19 CAP	18 AQU	19 ARI	18 TAU
19 LIB	20 SAG	21 AQU	20 PIS	21 TAU	20 GEM
21 SCO	22 CAP	23 PIS	22 ARI	23 GEM	22 CAN
24 SAG	24 AQU	25 ARI	24 TAU	25 CAN	25 LEO
26 CAP	26 PIS	27 TAU	26 GEM	27 LEO	27 VIR
28 AQU	28 ARI	29 GEM	29 CAN	30 VIR	30 LIB
30 PIS	30 TAU		31 LEO		

1989

JUL	AUG	SEP	OCT	NOV	DEC
2 CAN	3 VIR	1 LIB	1 SCO	2 CAP	2 AQU
4 LEO	5 LIB	4 SCO	4 SAG	5 AQU	4 PIS
6 VIR	8 SCO	6 SAG	6 CAP	7 PIS	7 ARI
9 LIB	10 SAG	9 CAP	9 AQU	9 ARI	9 TAU
11 SCO	12 CAP	11 AQU	11 PIS	11 TAU	11 GEM
14 SAG	15 AQU	13 PIS	13 ARI	13 GEM	13 CAN
16 CAP	17 PIS	15 ARI	15 TAU	15 CAN	15 LEO
18 AQU	19 ARI	17 TAU	17 GEM	17 LEO	17 VIR
20 PIS	21 TAU	19 GEM	19 CAN	20 VIR	19 LIB
23 ARI	23 GEM	21 CAN	21 LEO	22 LIB	22 SCO
25 TAU	25 CAN	24 LEO	23 VIR	25 SCO	24 SAG
27 GEM	28 LEO	26 VIR	26 LIB	27 SAG	27 CAP
29 CAN	30 VIR	29 LIB	28 SCO	30 CAP	29 AQU
31 LEO			31 SAG		

1990

JAN	FEB	MAR	APR	MAY	JUN
1 PIS	1 TAU	2 GEM	1 CAN	3 VIR	1 LIB
3 ARI	3 GEM	5 CAN	3 LEO	5 LIB	4 SCO
5 TAU	5 CAN	7 LEO	5 VIR	8 SCO	6 SAG
7 GEM	8 LEO	9 VIR	8 LIB	10 SAG	9 CAP
9 CAN	10 VIR	12 LIB	10 SCO	13 CAP	11 AQU
11 LEO	12 LIB	14 SCO	13 SAG	15 AQU	14 PIS
13 VIR	15 SCO	16 SAG	15 CAP	17 PIS	16 ARI
16 LIB	17 SAG	19 CAP	18 AQU	20 ARI	18 TAU
18 SCO	20 CAP	21 AQU	20 PIS	22 TAU	20 GEM
21 SAG	22 AQU	24 PIS	22 ARI	24 GEM	22 CAN
23 CAP	24 PIS	26 ARI	24 TAU	26 CAN	24 LEO
26 AQU	26 ARI	28 TAU	26 GEM	28 LEO	26 VIR
28 PIS	28 TAU	30 GEM	28 CAN	30 VIR	29 LIB
30 ARI			30 LEO		

1991

JAN	FEB	MAR	APR	MAY	JUN
1 LEO	2 LIB	2 LIB	3 SAG	2 CAP	1 AQU
4 VIR	4 SCO	4 SCO	5 CAP	5 AQU	4 PIS
6 LIB	7 SAG	6 SAG	8 AQU	7 PIS	6 ARI
8 SCO	9 CAP	9 CAP	10 PIS	10 ARI	8 TAU
11 SAG	12 AQU	11 AQU	12 ARI	12 TAU	10 GEM
13 CAP	14 PIS	14 PIS	15 TAU	14 GEM	12 CAN
16 AQU	17 ARI	16 ARI	17 GEM	16 CAN	14 LEO
18 PIS	19 TAU	18 TAU	19 CAN	18 LEO	16 VIR
20 ARI	21 GEM	20 GEM	21 LEO	20 VIR	19 LIB
23 TAU	23 CAN	22 CAN	23 VIR	22 LIB	21 SCO
25 GEM	25 LEO	25 LEO	25 LIB	25 SCO	23 SAG
27 CAN	27 VIR	27 VIR	28 SCO	27 SAG	26 CAP
29 LEO		29 LIB	30 SAG	30 CAP	29 AQU
31 VIR		31 SCO			

1990

JUL	AUG	SEP	OCT	NOV	DEC
1 SCO	2 CAP	1 AQU	1 PIS	2 TAU	1 GEM
4 SAG	5 AQU	3 PIS	3 ARI	4 GEM	3 CAN
6 CAP	7 PIS	6 ARI	5 TAU	6 CAN	5 LEO
9 AQU	9 ARI	8 TAU	7 GEM	8 LEO	7 VIR
11 PIS	12 TAU	10 GEM	9 CAN	10 VIR	9 LIB
13 ARI	14 GEM	12 CAN	11 LEO	12 LIB	12 SCO
15 TAU	16 CAN	14 LEO	14 VIR	15 SCO	14 SAG
17 GEM	18 LEO	16 VIR	16 LIB	17 SAG	17 CAP
19 CAN	20 VIR	19 LIB	18 SCO	20 CAP	19 AQU
21 LEO	22 LIB	21 SCO	21 SAG	22 AQU	22 PIS
24 VIR	25 SCO	24 SAG	23 CAP	25 PIS	24 ARI
26 LIB	27 SAG	26 CAP	26 AQU	27 ARI	26 TAU
28 SCO	30 CAP	29 AQU	28 PIS	29 TAU	28 GEM
31 SAG			30 ARI		30 CAN

1991

JUL	AUG	SEP	OCT	NOV	DEC
1 PIS	2 TAU	3 CAN	2 LEO	2 LIB	2 SCO
3 ARI	4 GEM	5 LEO	4 VIR	5 SCO	4 SAG
6 TAU	6 CAN	7 VIR	6 LIB	7 SAG	7 CAP
8 GEM	8 LEO	9 LIB	8 SCO	10 CAP	9 AQU
10 CAN	10 VIR	11 SCO	11 SAG	12 AQU	12 PIS
12 LEO	12 LIB	13 SAG	13 CAP	15 PIS	14 ARI
14 VIR	15 SCO	16 CAP	16 AQU	17 ARI	17 TAU
16 LIB	17 SAG	18 AQU	18 PIS	19 TAU	19 GEM
18 SCO	20 CAP	21 PIS	21 ARI	21 GEM	21 CAN
21 SAG	22 AQU	23 ARI	23 TAU	23 CAN	23 LEO
23 CAP	25 PIS	25 TAU	25 GEM	25 LEO	25 VIR
26 AQU	27 ARI	28 GEM	27 CAN	28 VIR	27 LIB
28 PIS	29 TAU	30 CAN	29 LEO	30 LIB	29 SCO
31 ARI	31 GEM		31 VIR		

1992

JAN	FEB	MAR	APR	MAY	JUN
1 SAG	2 AQU	3 PIS	1 ARI	1 TAU	2 CAN
3 CAP	4 PIS	5 ARI	4 TAU	3 GEM	4 LEO
6 AQU	7 ARI	8 TAU	6 GEM	5 CAN	6 VIR
8 PIS	9 TAU	10 GEM	8 CAN	8 LEO	8 LIB
11 ARI	12 GEM	12 CAN	10 LEO	10 VIR	10 SCO
13 TAU	14 CAN	14 LEO	12 VIR	12 LIB	13 SAG
15 GEM	16 LEO	16 VIR	15 LIB	14 SCO	15 CAP
17 CAN	18 VIR	18 LIB	17 SCO	16 SAG	17 AQU
19 LEO	20 LIB	20 SCO	19 SAG	19 CAP	20 PIS
21 VIR	22 SCO	23 SAG	21 CAP	21 AQU	22 ARI
23 LIB	24 SAG	25 CAP	24 AQU	24 PIS	25 TAU
25 SCO	27 CAP	27 AQU	26 PIS	26 ARI	27 GEM
28 SAG	29 AQU	30 PIS	29 ARI	28 TAU	29 CAN
30 CAP				31 GEM	

1993

JAN	FEB	MAR	APR	MAY	JUN
2 TAU	1 GEM	2 CAN	1 LEO	2 LIB	1 SCO
4 GEM	3 CAN	5 LEO	3 VIR	4 SCO	3 SAG
7 CAN	5 LEO	7 VIR	5 LIB	6 SAG	5 CAP
9 LEO	7 VIR	9 LIB	7 SCO	9 CAP	7 AQU
11 VIR	9 LIB	11 SCO	9 SAG	11 AQU	10 PIS
13 LIB	11 SCO	13 SAG	11 CAP	13 PIS	12 ARI
15 SCO	13 SAG	15 CAP	14 AQU	16 ARI	15 TAU
17 SAG	16 CAP	17 AQU	16 PIS	18 TAU	17 GEM
19 CAP	18 AQU	20 PIS	19 ARI	21 GEM	19 CAN
22 AQU	21 PIS	22 ARI	21 TAU	23 CAN	22 LEO
24 PIS	23 ARI	25 TAU	24 GEM	25 LEO	24 VIR
27 ARI	26 TAU	27 GEM	26 CAN	28 VIR	26 LIB
29 TAU	28 GEM	30 CAN	28 LEO	30 LIB	28 SCO
			30 VIR		30 SAG

1992

JUL	AUG	SEP	OCT	NOV	DEC
1 LEO	2 LIB	2 SAG	2 CAP	1 AQU	1 PIS
3 VIR	4 SCO	5 CAP	5 AQU	3 PIS	3 ARI
5 LIB	6 SAG	7 AQU	7 PIS	6 ARI	6 TAU
7 SCO	8 CAP	10 PIS	10 ARI	8 TAU	8 GEM
10 SAG	11 AQU	12 ARI	12 TAU	11 GEM	10 CAN
12 CAP	13 PIS	15 TAU	14 GEM	13 CAN	12 LEO
15 AQU	16 ARI	17 GEM	17 CAN	15 LEO	14 VIR
17 PIS	18 TAU	19 CAN	19 LEO	17 VIR	16 LIB
20 ARI	21 GEM	21 LEO	21 VIR	19 LIB	19 SCO
22 TAU	23 CAN	24 VIR	23 LIB	21 SCO	21 SAG
24 GEM	25 LEO	26 LIB	25 SCO	24 SAG	23 CAP
27 CAN	27 VIR	28 SCO	27 SAG	26 CAP	26 AQU
29 LEO	29 LIB	30 SAG	29 CAP	28 AQU	28 PIS
31 VIR	31 SCO				31 ARI

1993

JUL	AUG	SEP	OCT	NOV	DEC
2 CAP	1 AQU	2 ARI	2 TAU	1 GEM	3 LEO
5 AQU	3 PIS	5 TAU	4 GEM	3 CAN	5 VIR
7 PIS	6 ARI	7 GEM	7 CAN	5 LEO	7 LIB
10 ARI	8 TAU	10 CAN	9 LEO	8 VIR	9 SCO
12 TAU	11 GEM	12 LEO	11 VIR	10 LIB	11 SAG
15 GEM	13 CAN	14 VIR	13 LIB	12 SCO	13 CAP
17 CAN	15 LEO	16 LIB	15 SCO	14 SAG	15 AQU
19 LEO	17 VIR	18 SCO	17 SAG	16 CAP	18 PIS
21 VIR	19 LIB	20 SAG	19 CAP	18 AQU	20 ARI
23 LIB	21 SCO	22 CAP	22 AQU	20 PIS	23 TAU
25 SCO	24 SAG	24 AQU	24 PIS	23 ARI	25 GEM
27 SAG	26 CAP	27 PIS	27 ARI	26 TAU	28 CAN
30 CAP	28 AQU	29 ARI	29 TAU	28 GEM	30 LEO
	31 PIS			30 CAN	

appendix B

In the left wheel below, write your Sun sign in the segment of the wheel that includes the time you were born. Then, going counterclockwise, write the signs of the zodiac following your Sun sign in each succeeding section until you reach Segment 1. Whatever sign you fill in this segment is your ascendant.

For instance, if your Sun sign is Aquarius, and you were born at 9:43 P.M., you would write "Aquarius" in Segment 5, as shown below. Using the method described above, the sign you would fill in in Segment 1 would be Libra. Therefore, Libra would be your ascendant.

It's important to note that this is an *approximate* method, and there's always a slight possibility for error. If your rising-sign description is clearly wrong, check the description in the segment preceding and following Segment 1.

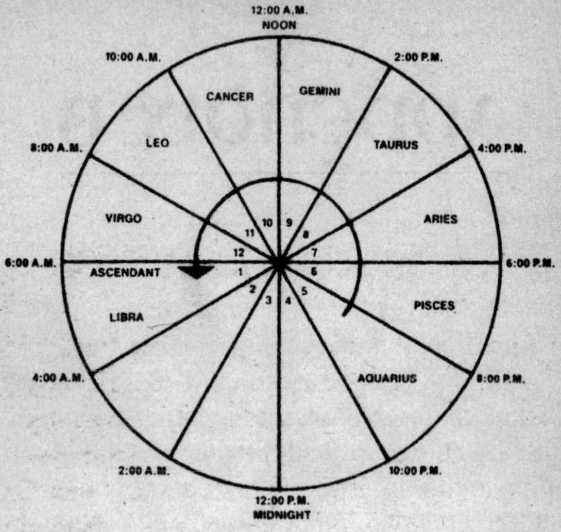
12:00 A.M.
NOON
2:00 P.M.
4:00 P.M.
6:00 P.M.
8:00 P.M.
10:00 P.M.
12:00 P.M.
MIDNIGHT
2:00 A.M.
4:00 A.M.
6:00 A.M.
8:00 A.M.
10:00 A.M.
CANCER
GEMINI
LEO
TAURUS
VIRGO
ARIES
ASCENDANT
LIBRA
PISCES
AQUARIUS
1
2
3
4
5
6
7
8
9
10
11
12

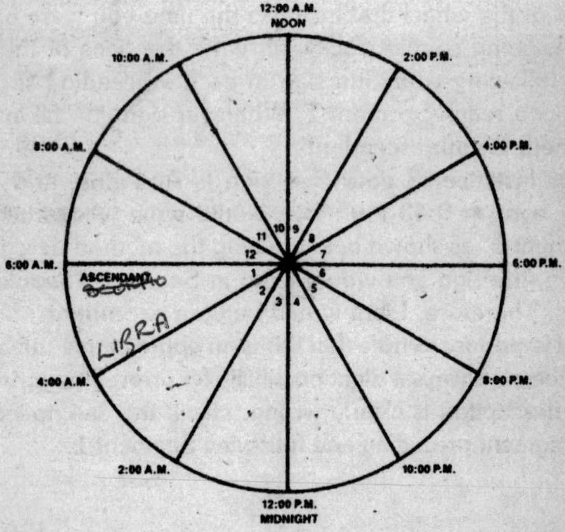
12:00 A.M.
NOON
2:00 P.M.
4:00 P.M.
6:00 P.M.
8:00 P.M.
10:00 P.M.
12:00 P.M.
MIDNIGHT
2:00 A.M.
4:00 A.M.
6:00 A.M.
8:00 A.M.
10:00 A.M.
ASCENDANT
LIBRA
1
2
3
4
5
6
7
8
9
10
11
12

ABOUT THE AUTHOR

Jonathan Sternfield, born in New York City, has lived in the Berkshires since 1969, residing in and around Great Barrington, Massachusetts. As a writer he has worked for the "College Bowl" television show, Rockefeller Center, and General Electric, among other clients. His published works include *The Complete Book of Mopeds* (Funk and Wagnall's), *The Berkshire Book* (Berkshire House Publishers), and many articles on electric cars and solar energy. He has also recently completed a New Age book, *Dawn of the Firewalkers*. As a photographer, he has worked for advertising agencies, actors, book illustrators, and rock videos. In his spare time, Jonathan Sternfield teaches tennis.

Nick

0621 - 742036.